Women Behind The Mic

Curators of Pop Culture

Volume 1

"Word To The Wise"

~Created, Compiled, and Edited by~

LaJoyce Brookshire & Michelle Joyce

Copyright 2023 © WOMEN BEHIND THE MIC – CURATORS OF POP CULTURE – VOLUME ONE – "WORD TO THE WISE"

By LaJoyce Brookshire & Michelle Joyce

PUBLISHER'S NOTE

Printed and bound in the United States of America. All rights reserved. No part of this book may be reproduced or transmitted in any form or by any means, electronic or mechanical, including photocopying, recording, video, streaming, or by any information storage and retrieval system except by a reviewer who may quote brief passages in a review to be printed in a magazine, newspaper, or on the Web without permission in writing from the publisher.

Although the author and publisher have made every effort to ensure the accuracy and completeness of information contained in this book, we assume no responsibility for errors, inaccuracies, omissions, or any inconsistency herein.

ISBN: 978-1-58441-006-5

RENEWING YOUR MIND INK

An Imprint of Peace in the Storm Publishing, LLC

Post Office Box 1152
Pocono Summit, Pennsylvania 18346
www.peaceinthestormpublishing.com

Dedication

This book is dedicated to anyone who has a Dream, and to anyone who wonders if a Dream is worth pursuing. Here are a collective of stories from Women who prove that Dream chasing is STILL worthwhile today.

Table of Contents

Foreword

"Women Behind The Mic"

-by-

David C. Linton

Chairman,
Living Legends Foundation Inc.

-and-

Program Director,

JAZZ 91.9 WCLK-FM / Clark Atlanta University

James Brown proudly proclaimed, "*This is a man's world, but it would be nothing without a woman or a girl*" in his classic song "This is A Man's World." For years we have heard the adage speak to the influence, power, and nurturing nature of women in society.

However, history and current times have shown us that women's roles are multi-dimensional and cannot be confined to any specific area. We do know that if we look hard enough, no matter what happens, there is a woman in the picture. Sometimes women have been stereotyped, especially, Black women or women of color, and not in a good way. Recently, Hollywood has taken it upon itself to "Recast" the role of women, but even in its recasting, women of color are the least celebrated.

I was delighted when Dr. LaJoyce Hunter Brookshire, my friend and former colleague from Arista Records, asked me to write something for the book you are about to read, and the phenomenal women highlighted in it. Many of these women have touched my life directly as a member of the music and broadcast industries. Some have been my colleagues at the biggest record labels in history. Others helped influence choices I have made in my career as both a radio broadcaster and music label executive. Whether you know it or not, they have influenced you as well due to their impact on Pop Culture.

They may not possess household names, but you know their work if you have ever read the credits on a TV show, album/CD cover, music video, or a press release about your favorite recording artists, then surely you may have come across their names. *Women Behind The Mic* is a collection of stories from what I like to call "The Star Makers." "The Mic" is a metaphor for behind-the-scenes. Everyone knows the Star, but few know those who really do the work to make the star shine.

Yes, the artist may have talent, and some don't, to be honest, but when these dynamic individuals put their polishing touch on them, they shine. The longevity is up to the artist, but these talented people will prepare them for their "15 Minutes of Fame."

Did you know the talent booker for the "World Famous Apollo Theater" in Harlem is a woman named Mary Flowers? If you love Aretha Franklin, Whitney Houston, Monica, and Freddie Jackson, to name a few, they all have in common a marketing director by the name of Jacqueline Rhinehart. If you grew up during the BET era and watched a show called *Teen Summit* or read the magazine *Sister2Sister,* then you know the name Jamie Foster-Brown.

How many times have you seen an artist or athlete give an interview you hated? Well, if you did, it's because they had not been media trained properly. Everyone's go-to person for media training their artists is Dyana Williams, a member of Radio's Hall of Fame, also known as "The Mother of Black Music Month!"

There are so many delightful stories that take you behind the scenes of the careers of artists like Prince, Queen Latifah, Sean "Puffy" Combs, Monica, Usher, and so many others. I don't want to continue naming names, but one thing I can say from working with many of these women is that they have mastered their crafts.

This is a book about struggle, survival, and triumph in a very brutal and not-so-friendly very male-dominated industry. This book will encourage you to follow your dreams, how to transition from one stage of life and/or career to another. You will find new "Sheroes," and you'll get a real understanding of what "Black Girl Magic" is all about. I am proud to invite you to read about these wonderful "Women Behind The Mic."

Preface

"We Won't Be Erased"

~by~

LaJoyce Hunter Brookshire

Photo Credit: Elijah (Farmer) Muhammad

When the history of Hip Hop and Pop Culture are told, it will be filled with gaping holes due to the missing pieces of the stories about the WOMEN BEHIND THE MIC. Here is a project that has been birthed due to this very fact.

In 2017, I specifically remember when the *New Edition Story* Biopic was going to air. I cleared my calendar, planned a week's worth of meals for dinner and TV snacking, and tried to contain my excitement as the airing date came near. You see, when the burgeoning New Edition was ascending, I was a full-time high school teacher and part of the working New York City Press Corps covering entertainment for the Sheridan Broadcasting Networks (now American Urban Radio Network AURN), *New York Beacon News*, and *Billboard* Magazine. My girl students were wearing me out, swooning over the group constantly! Back in the days of New Edition's beginnings, I was thrilled to interview them, review their albums, attend their concerts and luncheons, all thanks to Juanita Stephens, the label publicist at MCA Records and her ever-ready assistant Renee Foster.

I was soooo happy to know that the New Edition fellas were getting their stories told! It was during the 80s era when any young group of Black men, who were able to dodge the crack bullet, you were openly shouting, Hallelujah! I was equally filled with anticipation to see how my two sister-friends, Juanita and Renee, would be depicted on the screen.

The series was AMAZING! It was so well-done…beautifully scripted, beautifully filmed, and very detailed. As a mother, I was thrilled to see how the "Mamas" were featured front and center being advocates for their young stars. I was so impressed that the storyline aligned with all those conversations I had with the fellas over the years. However, as I sat in expectation in front of the television night after night, waiting for a glimpse, a mention, or a shred of evidence of the work put in by my Juanita and my Renee on that screen—the work which helped me to do MY work—I was sadly disappointed that my sisters were nowhere to be mentioned.

I was furious. I was South Side of Chicago spitting ANGRY! I thought about how much of an advocate Renee and Juanita were for New Edition—every day. Those ladies made sure the boys ate well, stayed in decent hotels, completed their studies, and even made sure they had condoms! And in a three-part mini-series with me spending six hours of my time glued to the TV—I enjoyed every minute of it. Until the stark realization hit me that my friends were glaringly absent.

Wait. What?

It reminds me of when I happily paid my own money and went to the movie theater in my country town on a Wednesday afternoon in 2009 to watch *Notorious*. I had my daughter situated at dance class for the afternoon, my popcorn, and my memories of having been BIG's publicist…until the last day of his life. Excited was definitely an understatement! And there it was…the moment that caused me to choke on my popcorn and cuss aloud at the screen. In the movie, during the ONE and only scene where the filmmakers could have shown that a Black woman was handling the publicity business of the moment, they chose to use a White man! I could not believe it. The man in the film did not say anything, but it was clearly made known HE was the one handling the publicity business.

I SCREAMED aloud, "Ohhhh…So, I'm a White man nowwwww!?!?!" throwing popcorn at the screen. Everyone in the theater turned to look at the person hurling hands of popcorn and screaming. I felt utterly erased. I got up and left because all I could see was red. I have never seen the entire movie, not even to this day.

The final straw was when *Can't Stop Won't Stop: A Bad Boy Story* documentary was released in 2017. My industry sister for life, Michelle Joyce called, and our conversation went like this:

"Did you see *Can't Stop Won't Stop*?" she asked.

"Yep."

"Did anyone call you to participate?"

"Nope. You?"

"Nope. And no one called Gwen, Leota, or Kelly either!"

"That is some messy mess. I'm tired."

"Me, too," she said.

Then, quietly, we got to work, and *Women Behind The Mic*™ was born. We contacted women from the Music Industry and asked every one of them to write their story. As the pages poured in during 2018, it was amazing to read all the outstanding accomplishments from this elite group of ladies whom I am honored to call my Sisters. We toiled in the trenches HARD. And just by doing our jobs, we realized that we have curated a little thing called Pop Culture. So much so that Hip Hop is now classified as Pop Culture as well!

We <u>DID</u> that! You may not know our names, but you know our work! This was satisfactory for me for a very long time, but not anymore. It is time our daughters and granddaughters know about the significant contributions that have been made to the Culture.

Women Behind The Mic™ is so much more than a book. It is a Movement to ensure we are not erased. There will be volumes of books to come, a Docu-Series, and a lecture series. We will tell our own stories because as Miriam Makeba says…

"The conqueror writes history, they came, they conquered, they write. You don't expect the people who came to invade us to tell the truth about us."

Mic Drop…Enough said.

Erasure

Noun

Pronounced: era-sure

: An act or instance of erasing

INTRODUCTION

"A Woman Did That"

~by~

Michelle Joyce

As I sat down to write this introduction, the word that came vividly to mind was 'erasure.' The stories are being told, the books are being written, the biopics are being filmed, and yet the stories are incomplete.

We were not 'hidden figures,' we were standing in plain sight. And so, with ***Women Behind The Mic,*** we are setting the story straight.

For centuries we have heard the term ***Behind Every Great Man Is A Woman.*** With this book series, lecture series, and Docu-series to come, we are flipping the script with the truth that is…***Beside Every Great Man Is An Equally Great Woman.***

These pages are a beautiful tapestry woven with the personal stories of the women who worked behind the scenes in the music industry. These women have played pivotal roles in shaping the sound and direction of what is known today as Popular music, yet their stories have remained largely untold.

This book is for anyone who wants a career in the music industry, to gain a deeper understanding of the music industry, and learn of the significant and often overlooked contributions of the women who shaped it.

As the reader, you will come to know the women who have broken barriers, shattered glass ceilings, built bridges where no bridge existed before, and blazed a trail for the next generation of female executives.

These are my Sisters, and these are their stories. ~MJ

WOMEN BEHIND THE MIC

"A Tribute"

Making deals Behind The Mic is her game,
And I bet, you don't even know her name,
...what a shame

Discovering and developing Stars for the stages,
Quietly earning those six figure wages.

She's in charge of the show and the flow,
and if you don't know, you'd never know!

She's the one in the room we need to mention,
Working that Black Girl Magic...So pay attention...

Classy, Sassy, Fabulous, and Fashiony.
Making moves Behind The Mic,
Working millions of Hits you know we like.

Sure, you can be a star and be done,
Question...have you got the skills it takes to make one?

They've built a strong and unique Sisterhood,
Planting them in the record books as history should.

Their contributions to this music game have been significant,
For decades they've moved in stealth mode...like the Syndicate.

Now the Behind-The-Scenes stories are about to be told in
truthfulness,

Through Books. Documentaries. Lectures...It's voluminous!
Asking yourself, "How Can I Be Down?",
Pay attention and stick around.

Stay Ready, so you don't have to Get Ready,
Is the best advice EVER!
Get some education for success of any future endeavor.

The only way to attain a seat at this table,
Is to put in that work to prove you're able.

What is the acumen Behind The Mic plight?
Ask the Women - and it will be done right.

Who cranked out the work on the songs you know we like?
Now you know, it was the Women Behind The Mic.

~LJB 1.23

Mic Check 1

"Watch The Magic"

~by~

Jacqueline Rhinehart

I fell in love with music at the age of five with the first album given to me, *Alice in Wonderland.* My first requested album was Sly & The Family Stone's *There's a Riot Going On.* I have a deep appreciation for music. And fortunately, I went to school when 'music appreciation' study meant something: A complete approach to the arts, music in particular. There was Music in school, in church, as a hobby—and all such activity was approached seriously—it was fun, but it was seriously fun. Our teachers were exquisite. I played the trumpet in high school and made third chair in All-State Band.

I also sang in the school choir; and was a founding member of the *Uplifters* our professional local choral group (think Kirk Franklin, et al.)

In addition, my brother played saxophone and keyboards in a professional band, touring the Southeast, at age 15, and due to the fact that everyone—I mean, virtually *everyone*—I knew played an instrument, or was in a band, or sang…I became that aficionado who also recognized and promoted excellent talent. It was natural because I was always surrounded by the best.

We listened to the best of wide variety—all genres of music: jazz, blues, rock, classical, soul, funk, R&B, gospel, pop. Growing up, music was crucial. Music provided the grid of our daily life. Sunday was Jazz. Weekday mornings were WOIC Radio and Bill Terrell at 6:00am. Saturdays were ironing sessions with Mom, potato chips, onion dip, *American Bandstand,* and *Soul Train.*

And rehearsal was ongoing. I had trumpet practice every day. Piano lessons on Saturday, choir practice and *Uplifters* practice… we were always playing music, listening to music, and consuming music.

The first music I loved was primarily instrumentals: "Listen Here" by Electrifying Eddie Harris; Sergio Mendes, "Brasil '66"; and "Down Here on the Ground" by Wes Montgomery.

Backing that general interest and love of music was my interest in the 'artwork' of music—the album covers.

I studied the art of packaging: photography, graphics, and public relations—the How-To of the music industry.

And I read EVERYTHING.

In addition, I incorporated music and the business of music into all the jobs I had. I worked as an overnight DJ at the Top-40 radio station, WNOK-FM. I worked as the advertising director for local record store. I worked as a runner for the major concert promotersm Don Jennings and Al Haymon. When I was appointed the Director of the South Carolina Governor's Mansion, I was also handling the booking for bands in my area, R&B and Jazz bands and placing them in many highly coveted venues—including the SC Governor's Mansion. I also created merchandising for many major recording artists while still living in South Carolina. Operating first as TRYAD and Jackie Productions Inc., my team and I created marketing events and merchandise for Rick James, Zapp/Roger Troutman, Prince, and others.

I worked in Public Relations for both politicians and musicians. True influence is compounded by a full-pronged attack in each endeavor, and it requires art, image, music, video, graphics, performance, and presentation.

The Debut—how an Artist is introduced—by whom and to whom—and all that is unveiled—that is the direct purview of the Chief Marketing Officer. And that was my dream. It all prepared me for a career in entertainment.

My greatest area of strength is my ability to EMPATHIZE with the Artist and the consumer. While I data is the lingua franca of marketing, it most often, for me, only reaffirms what I have instinctively understood. But it does provide infinite details.

Moving to New York City to fully explore working in the music industry was crucial. And living in Ft Greene, Brooklyn, was a blessing.

I have worked with seminal companies: Hush Productions, Arista Records, Uptown Records, Mercury Records, and Universal Records, to name a few. I have worked extensively in virtually every division of the music business. Primarily, I held positions in Marketing (product management), Publicity and Artist Development, and A&R. I left Universal label as Sr. Vice President of Marketing.

Some of the artists I have had the opportunity to work with are: Rick James, Zapp, George Clinton, Fatback Band, Cameo, Barkays, Kleeer, Kashif, Melba Moore, Freddie Jackson, Melisa Morgan, Alex Bugnon, Najee, McFadden & Whitehead, Ray Goodman & Brown, Jacci McGhee, Keith Sweat, BBD, TLC, Force MD's, Black Sheep, Jimmy Jam & Terry Lewis, Whitney Houston, Dione Warwick, Aretha Franklin, Lisa Stansfield, Oleta Adams, Jon Lucien, Toni Tony Tone, Vanessa Williams, Boyz II Men, Brian McKnight, Joe, Kem, Donnie, Toni Braxton, The Braxtons, Joi, Erykah Badu, Nelly, Master P, Mary J. Blige, Heavy D, Lil Romeo, Lil Wayne, Rakim, WingWang Twins, 8Ball & MG, Timberland, Q-Tip, Faith, Notorious B.I.G., Craig Mack, Monica, Murphy Lee, and Monifah; label launches for LaFace Records and Bad Boy.

All of these artists are superstars in their own right. They each exhibited an unusual/unique way to tell a common, yet rarely seen, truth. And they did it extremely well.

I took special interest in Monica, Lisa Stansfield, Erykah Badu, Nelly, Oleta Adams, Black Sheep, and Najee because their introductions were so crucial to their musical outcomes.

I felt the weight of helping to shepherd their first albums—there's a first time for everyone and Introductions are critical. The imprimatur was mine to set. They would be stars.

I am only frustrated with artists when they do not outfit their business staff with the same nuanced excellence as they do in their craft.

There were pivotal moments… One moment I recall warmly is when Lisa Stansfield received a standing ovation at the Apollo Theatre (to the relief of Arista president Clive Davis and the Arista staff—all fearful of possible rejection of the 'White girl' in the soul sanctuary). The other is

Rakim's comeback Gold double album (a double album set I pitched—and had to fight for—with label chairman Doug Morris).

When dealing with difficult situations I remember "Memento mori—remember you must die," and I speak with calm assuredness that we will all die—literally and metaphorically. So, Relax. Because those that refuse to support the life of a GREAT idea will also die, by the wayside, they die, too!

On the Job:

The most frustrating thing about my job was peer jealousy.

I respect the IDEA. I never push me—to do so is to engage in an argument to determine *who* is right. I debate ideas—the point is to determine the truth or *what* is BEST. And since that idea could be from either of us…the discussion is in the quest for the BETTER IDEA not the BETTER PERSON.

The aspect of the job that I enjoyed the most was IDEATION and Creation—Stand back and Watch the Magic!

My entire career points to some heavy successes.

Knowing that the artists whom I help to set their course are still relevant today is the most gratifying part.

To be reaffirmed that what you saw as indelible…it is especially gratifying when I hear them on the radio because they SOUND great! Particularly, the production quality of Hush Productions; absolutely brilliant production and sound engineering. As they say, 'Quality has no fear of time' and I worked only with the CLASSICS. They've been worthy of your time.

The Bugs:

Those who work in corporations with an aim to compete with their co-workers—not collaborate—are a pain in the ass to work with. Possibly today, new business models (due to tech disruptions) favor those that develop a culture of collaboration.

All else Karma will handle.

Fortunately, I have/had some beloved industry champions in Sidney Miller, Charles & Beau Huggins, Reggie Benson, and Von Alexander. While the most important survival skill that I could not do without in the business, is an infinite passion for the art—untarnished by melodrama.

Women have a secure place in history. But I understand that revisionist history is always taking place unless you are in the room when the story for a biopic is being conceived. We now must make history and publicize it as well! Oh, well...Hello Selfie!

Today, I would tell my younger self to know the difference between constituents, comrades, and confidantes—know their alignments. Keep confidant circles close and small. And although you may not do it for the money...take all the money you don't care about! Stay Cool. Have a Vision Board and eliminate scenes and people who don't serve your vision—always.

To younger women just getting started, I say, study, know and love the business—not any one personality in it. Avoid the illusion of loyalty to one person by standing true to what this is—the transmission ,protection and promotion of MUSIC and CULTURE.

I left the industry due to forced retirement visa vie label political machinations. The most useful skill I learned from the entertainment industry, applicable in any industry today, is the ability to see the intersection of one's industry and another (and another!).

I also gained the ability to recognize the keys to truly effective mass communication done efficiently. The principles to promote a message decisively, directly, and efficiently, that's the music biz - it's a primer on 'How to function on a large scale—with a small budget.'

Today I am the Head of Organic Soul Farm; Co-head Organic Soul Film & Entertainment; and Author, *My Organic Soul from Plato to Creflo, Emerson to MLK, Jesus to Jay-Z.*

And *still* making magic.

Jacqueline Rhinehart with Erykah Badu

Mic Check 2

"Talent Won't Be Denied"

~by~

Richelle Cross

Music was played on a daily basis in my home. I grew up listening to Motown artists along with gospel singers. Both my mother and grandparents loved music and dancing. I enjoyed music with lyrics that reflected my mood at any particular time. Music was my form of comfort whether I was happy, excited, bored, or sad. "Rapper's Delight" was the first Hip Hop song I fell in love with as a teenager. I recall taking the Paoli local train into Philly during high school (without my mother's permission) and meeting my best friend at the time, so we could see The Sugar Hill Gang perform live.

When I graduated from the University of Virginia with my degree in English, my original plan was a career as a sportswriter. My grandfather started teaching me sports when I was five years old. It was how we bonded. Unfortunately, a month after my college graduation, my grandfather passed away from cancer. In dealing with my grief, I turned down the job offer I had received to cover local sports. By the time I moved to Atlanta five years later, I was ready to find another niche. There was a job opening with an independent record label which primarily specialized in R&B and Blues. However, the owners decided it was time to venture into hip hop. I was initially hired as the Director of Publicity and less than a month later, I was asked to oversee Video Promotion as well. Music videos were a huge marketing tool due to the success of music video networks like BET, MTV, The Box and impactful local outlets like Video Music Box. I saw a path to be my own boss and started Class and Sass Video Promotions on January 17, 1992. My first three clients were LaFace, RCA, and Warner Music.

Over the last three decades, my company has developed and executed visual media campaigns for emerging, established and heritage artists in all genres of music. In the world of hip hop, I have been fortunate to promote and work with Ice Cube, Queen Latifah, Scarface, Rakim, Heavy D, Diddy, Biggie, Lil Wayne, Drake, Nicki Minaj, DJ Khaled, Nelly, Birdman, Outkast, and Juvenile to name a few.

One of my biggest strengths which has contributed to my company's longevity is my passion for what I do. I don't accept projects that I don't believe in just to get a check. I won't promote music videos which offend me as a woman or as a mother. My integrity means everything to me.

The most successful artists are the ones who have a keen understanding of who they are and refuse to allow the record label to portray them differently. Other successful acts have such an incredible work ethic that there's little doubt their efforts will be rewarded. But the true superstars and legends in the game have a talent that simply cannot be denied. It's in their swagger, their wordplay and how their mere presence takes over the room or stage. Biggie had it. Wayne has it. Nicki has it.

Cash Money Records (and subsequently, Young Money Entertainment) has been a client for 25 years. Despite the success of Juvenile's debut album, *400 Degreez*, and the platinum and gold albums that followed by their other acts, it took the industry way too long to recognize the independent label as a major player. Everyone on the team had to work extremely hard for their artists to receive the recognition they deserved. On the video side, it was easy to obtain video airplay, but I had to fight hard for them to appear on the music video award shows. Nevertheless, all of that resistance went away with the release of Lil Wayne's *Tha Carter III*.

When I first started working in this industry, it was frustrating trying to work with certain men who held prominent positions at the record labels who didn't respect women. I was propositioned a lot. They didn't care that I was married and I didn't have a problem telling their butts NO. As a result, there were accounts I was unable to obtain. But if I am to be totally honest, one of the most disheartening things that I've experienced is the jealousy and backstabbing by other women especially the ones whom I tried to help and uplift. So I've learned to be very cautious about who I let into my inner circle.

Without question, the three biggest industry mentors whom I have had during this journey are Miller London, Jean Riggins and Jackie Rhinehart. Miller was one of my first clients (RCA) and went out of his way to introduce me to other executives when I started my company. Jean and Jackie welcomed my ideas and encouraged me. They helped me to find my voice and freely shared their stories and wisdom. I also have colleagues like Rhonda Cowan, Lynn Scott, Kira Daniels and Tuma Basa to offer advice and support whenever it is needed.

Nothing is more rewarding than seeing an artist whose project I've worked on be celebrated on a national stage or the artist's joy when their album is certified platinum. I am extremely proud of the work we've accomplished with so many artists that it's hard to select one. The three major standouts would be working with Bad Boy, Nelly, and of course, Young Money/Cash Money.

I knew that Class and Sass Video Promotions was a success when I no longer had to reach out to labels for business. Folks were contacting us and offering this Black owned company projects to promote in all genres. I knew BET and MTV respected the clients I had when they sought me out to book appearances and performances. Nevertheless, I don't feel most women are recognized for their work in this male dominated industry. We are rarely shown in biopics and documentaries and very few artists acknowledge our efforts publicly. Hell, I've watched a slew of folks take credit for my work. Sometimes I check them and other times, I simply smile. In the end, I know what I've done and that's all that truly matters.

I would tell young women embarking in this industry to be passionate, always be willing to learn, and don't be afraid to take risks. Also, it's important to learn the art of networking. It's probably the one thing that I didn't do enough because I wanted to isolate myself from the daily b.s. and fake people in the business.

Class and Sass Promotions celebrated its 30th anniversary in 2022. Our company continues to excel with providing a plethora of visual media opportunities for our clients within the traditional music video space as well as increasing artist visibility and outreach thru non-music programming. Over the last decade, our clients have appeared on ESPN, Fox Sports, Bravo and Inside The NBA along with numerous podcasts. In 2019, we co-produced two films for BET as well as a Breast Cancer anthology special for BET Her. Lastly, we worked with Young Money and the National Museum of African American Music (NMAAM) to curate an exhibit on Lil Wayne, making him the first rapper to be featured in the museum.

After more than three decades, I am blessed to still be in the game.

Richelle Cross with Lil Wayne

Mic Check 3

"Responsibility Comes with That Mic"

~by~

Dyana Williams

Photo Credit: Whitney Thomas

I had a lot of jobs prior to the entertainment industry as a young teenager because I was a worker. My first radio job was in New York at WBAI, which is a listener-supported radio station for Pacifica. I used to sit in for a gentleman named Rob Crocker, and this was after I had done my radio show at the carrier current station at City College of New York in Harlem. I caught the radio bug, and Rob allowed me to sit in for him when he was off. We did a jazz show. That was it. I was very clear on what I was going to do from a very young age.

One day, somebody invited me up to the carrier-current radio station on the City College campus in New York City to meet them, and I didn't even know the college had a radio station. But I walked in and saw the turn tables, microphones, the dial switches, everything. I just got excited and enamored, and that settled for me. I enrolled in a course to learn the basics, and shortly thereafter, I got my own jazz radio show. I love jazz music. That was the beginning for me, and at that point, I was 18. I decided, somewhere during that first year of college, that I wanted to drop out and get a job as a radio personality. Much like my first inspiration in radio, Ms. Vy Higginsen, who was on WBLS-FM—107.5 in New York City. Those were the early days of my broadcasting aspirations and career. My first full-time job in radio was at WHUR-FM - 96.3 in Washington DC, a commercial radio station owned by Howard University. I was hired on the eve of my 19th birthday by Bob "NightHawk" Terry... he was a colorful and talented disc jockey/programmer featured in a film called *Talk to Me*. He heard an audition tape and resume that I had sent in pursuit of an on-air position. WHUR was my first full-time making money every week, and a job "with-health-benefits" in broadcasting.

City College is where I learned the basics running the board in radio. Then I took those skills to a career. It all built my confidence, and I had a mentor, Van Jay. He [Jay] was on the air at WRVR FM, which was the straight-ahead jazz station in New York in the early '70s. He was on late nights, and I used to listen to him when I was doing my schoolwork. So, I called him one night on the listener's request line and said I'm on the air at WCCR. I told him that I was going to be on the radio and famous one day. I also told him, "I'm not a get coffee girl. I'm coming in to learn. If you're amenable, then I'll visit." Van teased me for years, he said, "Girl, I knew you was going someplace."

I dropped out of college, got the job at WHUR, and didn't look back. I've worked in radio since. Then I did a stint in DC, as Ebony Moonbeams; that was my radio handle.

When I joined the staff at 96.3 WHUR-FM, I became the third on-air personality, after Alfie, Williams and Dianne Quander. Dianne would go on to write the lyrics for Anita Baker's classic "Caught Up in the Rapture". I stayed a couple of years and developed a very strong following, eventually moving to mid-days. We're talking about Chocolate City, the nation's capital when it was Black; it was very, very Black.

While I was on the air at WHUR, I got a phone call from one of the preeminent broadcast programmers and radio personalities of all time, Frankie Crocker. He offered me a job, first, in St. Louis. I was 20 at the time, my mother and I went to St. Louis, and it was just not for me. I grew up in Harlem, a very fast-paced cosmopolitan city, and DC was that as well. So, I said no to St. Louis. Then he offered me a job in Chicago and a lot of money, and the owners called me back to say sorry, we cannot pay you what Mr. Crocker offered you. I thought, *okay, I guess I won't be going to Chicago.* Finally, Frankie called me back and said come to New York, come to WBLS.

When I was 18, I wrote a list of goals, and among those was to return to my hometown and get a job in radio. So, there I was, 21 when Frankie Crocker brought me to New York, and WBLS. My parents, the people I grew up with, my family, people I had gone to college with and knew that I had dropped out were able to hear me every day on the radio. I did an over-night shift. That was pretty heavy, to be 21 on the radio in New York City, in my hometown, doing my thing. I was thrilled and doing it with Frankie Crocker, who was the best.

Worked at WBLS from 1975-1977, when I finally handed in my resignation. I left WBLS-FM in New York, when Kenny Gamble and I expected our first child son Caliph (we would have two more children Isa Salahdeen and Princess Idia in the following years). Kenny was the man of my dreams, and he happened to be one of the most successful songwriter/producers at that time in the music industry with Philadelphia International Records. He and his partner, Leon Huff, are the architects of the sound of Philadelphia. While we were deeply in love, we would later go our separate ways, but co-parented well together along with my children's bonus mother and Kenny's current wife, Faatimah Gamble. I respect Gamble as the head of our family and a dear friend to this day. I left WBLS because I devoted myself for a year to being a mother, breastfeeding, and making baby food from scratch, but I still loved radio and wanted to get back to work.

Despite the fact that my man did not want me to work and told me I didn't need to work, I was like, oh no, I need and love radio. I have little antennas in my vein! So, after moving back to DC and a year of being a full-time momma, I went back to work. I was offered a job in rock radio; there were very few women at that time, and even fewer Black and Latina women (I am Afro-Rican, my mother is Puerto Rican, and my father was Black). So, here I was, working at a rock station—WRQX. It was an ABC affiliate, so I was excited because now I was working with a network affiliation and doing rock radio. I prided myself then, as I still do, that I could do classical, country… you name it! Whatever, I can do any format. The format that I existed in for the majority of my career is Black radio playing soul music and R&B music. But yes, rock radio, and that was an experience.

Shortly after, I got pregnant with my second son and gave birth in 1978 to Isa Salahdeen Gamble. Then I heard about a TV station doing auditions for a correspondent for their new show called *P.M. Magazine*. When I was in college, I hosted an access-cable TV show called *Ebony Moonbeams*, which is where I got my handle from when I went to DC Two hundred people auditioned for this role, and I was blessed up again to get the job. That was WDVM-TV, and it's now WUSA in DC. TV and radio have been concurrent in my career from the beginning. I had incredible experiences learning how to write for TV, edit, produce. You know, I did it all.

I moved to Philadelphia full time in 1980 when WDAS-FM 105.3 General Manager, Cody Anderson and program director, Joe "Butterball" Tamburro offered me an on-air position. I did a weekend show called "Love's On the Menu", named after a song written by Jerry Butler. I did that for nearly ten years at WDAS. I was very into the community because I believe that when you're on the air, you are broadcasting to the Black community, there is a responsibility and an obligation that comes with being on that microphone. That is to superserve the community. That means being out at the churches, the nonprofits, the schools, NAACP, Urban League, hosting events, speaking to students and senior citizens everywhere - just being in the trenches with the everyday folk who support your outlet.

I worked ten years at WDAS, and it has a special place in my heart. The irony of it is I was on the air at a time when Gamble and Huff just dominated Black radio with the O'Jay's, Harold Melvin and the Blue Notes, Teddy Pendergrass, Phyllis Hyman, Jean Carne, The Three Degrees, The Jones Girls, and I was playing all of that music. I'd be home with Gamble, and he'd write the songs, go in the studio, record 'em, release 'em on Philadelphia International Records, and it went straight onto the turn tables at WDAS. It was exciting to play music, some of which were inspired by our relationship, our family, and our love.

When I left WDAS, I linked up with a friend of mine I had met at Howard University's radio station, Sheila Eldridge. Sheila was in marketing and PR, that was her strength not mine, but she had a company, Miles Ahead Entertainment and we started working together. In 1991, we established the International Association of African American Music (I.A.A.A.M.), and also created a foundation with that same name. It was inspired after going to a reckless Jack The Rapper Music conference in Atlanta, that just had devolved into a Sodom & Gomorrah type of situation. At the conference Jack's wife called the police because she knew it was out of control. I mean, there were strippers, chairs being thrown, and it was horrible. We were disgruntled, because we were serious women in the music industry that also came from the Black Music Association, and we were like, "Nah, this is not how you do it." So, we decided to establish I.A.A.A.M. instead of talking about things that were wrong and complaining, we said, "we will do it ourselves" and create a music conference that is consumer-based for the people who buy the music and support the industry with music industry professionals.

So, in 1991, Sheila and I produced the first I.A.A.A.M. celebration to recognize June nationally as "Black Music Month," and that [Black Music Month] was established on June 7, 1979, on the lawn of the White House with President Jimmy Carter. He hosted an event that featured Chuck Berry, Evelyn Champagne King, Sarah Powell, and Andraé Crouch. That was the first Black Music Month celebration, and we decided to make our event in June to recognize a month that I had worked on establishing with my ex, Gamble. For 16 years straight, we did the music conference every June. For several years, we also did it concurrently in London and expanded, again, the name of our company International Association of African-American Music. We wanted it to be an advocacy and educational organization that promoted and perpetuated Black music.

Sheila and I are no longer partners, but I've continued to be involved in the promotion and perpetuation of Black music. I wrote President Bill Clinton (we decided to do our I.A.A.A.M. Conference in DC) and I asked him if he could host an event similar to what Jimmy Carter had done in 1979. The White House wrote back and said, well, we see that Jimmy Carter hosted this event for Black Music Month, but he didn't sign a presidential proclamation. We were in shock, it was like we had been walking around for month's saying "Do Black Music Month!," and it was as far as we were concerned in the industry. But the White House asked for legislation.

Well, I comprehended what that meant, and put on some real comfortable flat shoes, and started going office-to-office in DC lobbying Congressman and Senators asking them to support a bill that would recognize the sizable contributions of African Americans in the multi-billion dollar music industry. I had assistance from Senator Arlen Specter from Pennsylvania, a Republican, who is no longer with us; and former Congressman Chaka Fattah, who was the primary advocate and introduced the draft that I wrote called the African American Music Bill. In 2000, I got the call from Lydia Sermons that the bill had passed in the House of Representatives. So, of course I was very excited, and I went back to the White House and said look! It's official, Congress said do the Black Music Month. I took a delegation of people to the White House, and I had a private meeting in the Oval Office with Sheila, Jeff Sharp (who was a concert promoter), who also was our partner in promoting an event at the Warner View Theater in DC at that time, and we met with Bill Clinton. We talked about the issues that are pertinent to our industry and working on getting regard with respect. Not just for our business as a cultural asset, but also a very viable aspect of commerce in America and globally. That was our first meeting in the Oval Office with President Clinton, it was worth every office that I went in, all the miles that I walked, all the emails, I wrote an editorial in *Billboard* Magazine for J.R. Reynolds, who was the then-Black music editor, he gave me tremendous support. We got the legislation passed in 2000, and that was a very happy and exciting time for us. I then took a delegation to the White House, with Jimmy Jam, Terry Lewis, Jamie Foster Brown, Teddy Pendergrass, Karen White, Ray Harris; many of us went to the White House repeatedly for events, meetings, and discussions about how we could elevate those who worked in the music industry. I count the establishment of June as Black Music Month one of my greatest accomplishments.

Then, I went into artist management for a period of time, with an artist/producer named Gary Taylor who was signed to Virgin Records.

Sharon Heyward was the president of Black music for the label. That's where I forged my friendship with Sharon. One day she takes me to lunch and says, "You should do artist development. You like artists, they like you. You have a way with them, you've been on the radio, you've been a manager, you would be an excellent artist development coach." At the time I didn't quite understand everything involved in artist development, but I knew it already, because I'd been involved in the music industry with Gamble and all of the Philadelphia International artists. Plus, with being on the radio and interviewing people all the time, I was ready. I began "Influence Entertainment."

My company was launched through artist development and media coaching, and entertainment services in the business. But I credit Sharon Heyward with being the person that recognized something new, something about me that I didn't know, but was real.My first coaching job was with Jimmy Jam and Terry Lewis's Perspective Records, with a group called Solo. My second client was Veritcal Hold featuring Angie Stone. My next client was an emerging superstar named D'Angelo, who remains one of my most cherished friends to this day; publicist Karen Taylor hired me to work with him. My phone hasn't stopped ringing since. I've been coaching over three decades now. I've been fortunate to work with numerous gifted artists in all genres, from Rihanna to Kirk Franklin to members of the Dave Matthews Band to Jack Harlow. In addition to recording artists, our client list includes actors, executives, atheletes, authors and social media influencers. Our roster is rather diverse! My team of coaches and producers include, K. Foxx, Daysha Screven and Laiya St. Clair.

That has been a blessing because Sharon is right, I have the capacity to empower people, to impart information in a way that they receive it and more often than not implement it and many of my clients have had successful careers. I can't take credit for all of their careers being successful because they were already talented, they had skill sets that obviously record companies and agents recognized, but I have contributed to the process. I'm proud of that.

The advice I would give to younger women looking to embark on a career in this industry is to understand that when you carry a don't-mess-with-me-attitude, people are less likely to try it. Even if you're scared or frightened, just carry some of that energy and people will be less likely to tamper with you. I can be playful, but I'm real serious about what I'm doing. I am very serious about the business of music; I was very serious about my career and about our community. So, you can try it if you'd like, but be prepared to get a tongue-lashing. I know how to do a cuss-out without using profanity. I am a verbal assassin.

Today, I am an active in my grandson's lives. I love my grandsons, Luke Gamble, and Nafis Lee! I am still doing life/media coaching for high profile individuals via my company, Influence Entertainment Influenceentertainment.com. I've been an on-camera commentator on TV One's NAACP Award winning music documentary series, *UNSUNG* since 2008. Currently, I am celebrating my 50th anniversary as a broadcaster and was nominated for the Radio Hall of Fame in 2022. Radio being my first professional love, I am on air contributor on 900am/96.1 WURD-FM Progressive Black Talk Radio in Philadelphia. For years I was the co-producer of the Marian Anderson Award, where I helped to orchestrated tributes honoring Jon Bon Jovi, Wynton Marsalis, Patti LaBelle, Kool & The Gang, Gamble & Huff. Additionally, I am a live event producer for the "Welcome America" Festival in Philadelphia. I have co-curated with Laiya St. Clair several art exhibitions featuring artist, Yusef Jaleel in Philadelphia, and the works of photographer Ron St. Clair in Nashville. It was amazing to be featured in the *New York Times* Arts & Leisure section. As a I've increased paid public speaking engagements with clients such as: Spotify, Tidal, and the Country Music Association!

I serve on the boards of the Recording Academy also known as the GRAMMYs, Temple University's Klein College of Media and Communication (where I delivered the commencement speech for the class of 2022) and the National Museum of African American Music in Nashville, Tennessee.

While I am still having a meaningful career, I want to encourage young folks to pursue their passion, identify a mentor, absorb as much information and experience as you can, netweave with professionals and create balance in your pursuits, personal and professional. Live life fully, with excellence as your focus and you will thrive. You will shine, be noticed and opportunities will come to you!

Dyana Williams with Chaka Khan

Mic Check 4

"Manage Relationships and Expectations"

~by~

Janine Coveney

Most people in the industry first got to know me as the R&B Music Editor at *Billboard* Magazine from 1989 to 1993 under my then-married name Janine McAdams. I've worked for other publications, including *Essence, R&B Airplay Monitor, The Gavin Report*, and *Impact,* and spent years writing for United Stations Radio Networks. I continue to write as an entertainment and lifestyle freelancer.

I fell in love with music as a child because of my parents. Dad loved classical, jazz, and soul. Mom loved Caribbean, Latin, Broadway, and pop. On Saturdays, cleaning day, my sisters and I often woke up to Tchaikovsky's "Swan Lake" or "The 1812 Overture," or my mother's Mighty Sparrow or Miriam Makeba sides, before the afternoon's sounds segued to Cannonball Adderley, Aretha Franklin, Nancy Wilson, Quincy Jones, Dionne Warwick, or Herb Alpert's Tijuana Brass. This is just a short list. They played music all day on the weekends; I studied the album cover art and read every word of the credits and liner notes as I listened. Music's ability to speak to our emotions, to invoke imagination and spark memory, to set the mood and offer solace, have always been important to me. I was into poetry as a kid, so I have a good memory for lyrics and an enduring respect for strong lyricists.

Growing up I was always singing, to the radio, to myself. I still do. The only kind of music that I wasn't regularly exposed to was country, but even so we'd occasionally have "Hee-Haw" on TV, and I would become mesmerized by Dolly Parton and Loretta Lynn. I had a lot of music-minded friends through church, and the guys who weren't into sports were budding musicians or party DJs. We would verbally dissect albums by the Isley Brothers, Return to Forever, Osibisa, Earth Wind & Fire, Fania All Stars, The Ohio Players, Steely Dan, and Mandrill in depth. We liked pop and soul music too, but we were about analyzing drum patterns, bass techniques, the architecture of vocal harmonies, well-placed horn hits. We wanted to understand the elements of good music.

Growing up in The Bronx, I got a front-row seat to how my beloved disco music morphed into Hip Hop. The biggest breakthrough was "Rapper's Delight", but I think it was Grandmaster Flash & the Furious Five with "The Message" and "White Lines" that I liked best. These songs spoke to the despair and struggle of people of color in the boroughs of New York and ultimately everywhere at that time. I saw the devastating effects of drugs, urban blight, unemployment, gangs, teen pregnancy and hunger had on my neighborhood. A lot of the neighbors on my block lost children to violence and drugs.

I never planned a career in music; I just knew I loved it. Though I was neither a great singer nor musician, as a teen I spent a lot of time in choirs, pick up bands, and in music lessons (piano, clarinet, flute). At 16 I got a job as a page at the Rodgers & Hammerstein Archive at the New York Public Library at Lincoln Center; this was an underground stash of every commercial recording ever released up to that time. The recordings could only be listened to on site. I read as many covers and listened to as much as I could while it was slow. No, I knew I was going to be a writer. It's all I ever wanted to do, as I was fascinated by storytelling and narrative. But music also carries that narrative function, and I learned early how to truly listen to a piece of music. I think that habit of careful listening, exposure to a lot of styles of music, combined with critical thinking and writing ability, have really helped me in my career.

I graduated from Simmons College in Boston with a degree in Advertising & Public Relations, planning to go into copywriting. I produced YA novels at Scholastic Inc. after college, then wrote about careers and home furnishings on the editorial staff at *Essence* Magazine. I landed at *Billboard* Magazine in the fall of 1987 as a copyeditor. I was thrilled because I had always loved music and kept up with artists, players, producers, lyrics, etcetera.

MUSIC INDUSTRY INTRO

Billboard was my real introduction to the music industry. At that time, the weekly magazine featured serious trade news for business insiders, it wasn't the glossy mag featuring fashion and pop culture stories that it has become now. Reading and editing the other reporters' stories gave me an in-depth education about all aspects of the music industry: Touring, record production, distribution, audio and video technology, music video production, pop, country, jazz, retail, and radio.

I was named R&B Music Editor for *Billboard* in June 1989, and I was ecstatic. I wasn't just dealing with newsgathering; now I had landed smack in the middle of a nationwide community of music people at a time when Black music was taking over *Billboard*'s pop sales and airplay charts. I had always chased stories at *Essence*, now stories were chasing me. I received dozens of letters from industryites I had yet to meet, congratulating me. Publicists rang my phone all day, pitching stories. Invitations overflowed my inbox. It was overwhelming.

My job was to gather and write news items, feature stories, reviews, and a weekly column. I covered R&B, Hip Hop, Smooth Jazz, Caribbean music, and Black rock. The scope of my coverage began to change as *Billboard* added hip-hop editor Havelock Nelson and a new editor in chief Timothy White, author of the Bob Marley bio Catch A Fire, blocked me from covering reggae in 1992.

The head of *Billboard's* Black Music charts was Ms. Terri Rossi, an industry powerhouse in her own right. God love her, she did everything in her power to champion me and introduce me to as many people as she could. I assumed the job in June of 1989; in August I headed to the Atlanta Airport Marriott to attend the Jack The Rapper Family Affair convention, my first music confab of any kind. When I tell you I was not prepared, I mean I was not prepared!! There were so many people and so much information. Apparently there had not been a Black woman editor at *Billboard* for a few years, not since Jean Williams had served the magazine in the 1960s and 70s, so Terri and a number of other music industry ladies (Dyana Williams, Jalila Larsuel, Juanita Stephens, Glynice Coleman, Cynthia Badie, Sheila Eldridge, Simo Doe, Ornetta Barber, Sharon Heyward, Linda Haynes, Mary Moore, Sarah Melendez, Ann Carli, Sandra Trim-DaCosta, Felicia Feeney, Sharon Washington, Maye James, Cassandra Mills, Karen Kennedy, Vonnie Sweeney, and others I'm sure I'm forgetting) organized a welcome reception for me. I was expecting a small polite gathering. I did not realize that *Billboard*'s publisher and several staff members as well as folks from every label and every aspect of the Black music industry would be there: publicity, promotion, A&R, music publishing, major labels, indie labels, songwriters, producers, radio programmers—all in the room. A&M, Def Jam, PolyGram, Jive, RCA, MCA, Arista, Cold Chillin', Wing, Tommy Boy, Columbia, Epic, Verve, Priority, Sleeping Bag, Orpheus, Motown, Capitol, Interscope, Ichiban, Virgin, Mercury, Relativity, Warner Bros., Loud, Polydor, Island—these were all viable labels at the time with entire staffs of folks. (LaFace was in its infancy, Bad Boy was 4 years away, and so was Death Row.)

The gig wasn't just researching and writing articles, it was also managing relationships and expectations for coverage. I think my greatest strengths as an editor were good ears, critical thinking, and a sense of fairness. I tried to find diplomatic ways to offer criticism, but I wasn't always successful. What I loved about the gig was the fact that every day was different, and that I was able to deal with people across the length and breadth of the industry. There were label-sponsored luncheons, cocktail parties, screenings, concerts, club performances, and video shoots to attend. I traveled a lot: Atlanta, Miami, New Orleans, Minneapolis, Los Angeles. It was nearly impossible to confine work to a 9 to 5 day, and after a while I stopped wanting to. It was hard work, but it was fun, too.

THE UPSIDE

It was an interesting time to get into the industry because the 1990s saw major changes. The lines between Black music and pop music were starting to disappear. Hip-hop now took over the music sales and airplay charts, it launched new labels and strengthened others. Most R&B singles now had to have a guest rapper on board. In the early 90s, dancehall also gained a big foothold on the charts. It was also the age of vocal groups, compilation soundtracks and top-billed production teams. *Billboard* itself was forced to re-evaluate the nomenclature for its charts, flipping from "R&B," which clearly indicated traditional rhythm & blues singing, to "Black Music" to encompass all forms of music being played on urban radio, which now included R&B, hip-hop, dancehall, and even smooth jazz. The major labels all launched fully staffed Black music divisions and rewarded its stalwarts with bigger executive titles and more perks. I remember doing a front-page story in 1991 about the appointments of all the new black music VPs and Presidents. Nielsen SoundScan was born in 1991, impacting piece-count data at retail outlets and regulating sales figures. Nielsen's Broadcast Data Systems airplay detection system, which ID'ed songs on the radio, launched in 1992. This meant a little less wiggle room for labels trying to manipulate the charts. These were all ongoing stories with widespread impact on the industry.

Some of the stories I was proudest of had to do with the ascendancy of hip-hop, the influence of rap on the culture at large, the influx of African American music video directors, the renewed popularity of girl groups (led by En Vogue, SWV, Total, Xscape, TLC, et al), the backlash against Ice-T's Body Count for "Cop Killer" and NWA for "F--- the Police," and subsequent efforts by radio to bleep out objectionable language while still playing the hits.

I was fortunate to have mentors. I owe Nelson George a debt of gratitude. The example he set as a thoughtful chronicler of not just the business, but of the music and personalities involved, provided the template for the kind of music journalist I wanted to be. When I arrived at the magazine, he assigned me stories that allowed me to grow into my role as section editor once he left the R&B Editor post.

It was the women in the industry who really went to bat for me, starting with Terri Rossi at *Billboard*; and particularly air personality and entrepreneur Dyana Williams and marketing/PR/media guru Sheila Eldridge, who together during their partnership in IAAAM, and separately, have advised me and given me numerous opportunities. Thanks to them I have written awards show scripts, appeared on

BET, traveled, spoken on industry panels, and was recommended for numerous writing gigs. I am grateful also to Sylvia Rhone, still the highest-ranking black woman in the industry; while it was known that she disliked interviews, she usually gave me access, and later offered me a job at Atlantic (that I'm sorry now I didn't take).

THE DOWNSIDE

One big challenge for me personally was that sexism—and misogyny—was also alive and well in the industry, and particularly within the culture of hip-hop. The lyrics of the records themselves often treated women as sex objects and side issues, and that attitude could permeate the attitudes of the folks who promoted the records. I had interviews with male artists who tried to manhandle or proposition me and incidents with their male handlers who did the same. I had to lay down the law in some situations, but in others I probably tolerated inappropriate language and behavior just to get along. I'm not saying that was the smartest way to handle things, but that's how I dealt with the issue. The industry was still male dominated, as was the management at *Billboard*, and I didn't want anyone to think that because I was a woman, I couldn't do my job. I remember writing a column after coming back from a Black Radio Exclusive conference in New Orleans, noting the rampant sexism in the industry and getting a lot of positive feedback about it.

The changes in the music industry—the gutting of the label system, massive layoffs, the tolerance for more raw subject matter in the music, the decline of music trade magazines, and the hailing of mediocre talents as the next big thing—have often made me want to quit writing about music altogether. But you become conditioned to looking to music as a gauge of our culture and a connection to what is happening now. Music still connects us, so it is hard to "quit."

When I left *Billboard* in May of 1993, I worked a mere six months at Arista Records, where I got to work with Whitney Houston, Aretha Franklin, TLC, Dionne Warwick, Toni Braxton, and others. I then grabbed the opportunity to move to Los Angeles in January 1994 to work as a publicist for Jimmy Jam & Terry Lewis' Perspective Records for a year. The label staff was heavily female, as the president was industry veteran Sharon Heyward, and my immediate boss was first Juanita Stephens (publicist extraordinaire and onetime manager of Bobby Brown) and then Sheila Eldridge. There I worked with Barry White, Gerald Levert (he managed a girl group called Drama on our roster), CeCe Peniston, Sounds of Blackness, and Mint Condition. I didn't enjoy working on the label side as much; I was too much of an introvert and too used to the writer's life.

I switched back into publishing, as managing editor of the short-lived radio magazine *Billboard Airplay R&B Monitor* (1995-1998), then as an editor at *Gavin* (1998-1999) and Impact (1999), then wrote entertainment news for syndicated radio services Launch then United Stations Radio Networks (2000-2010). My last fulltime gig was as Content & Communications Manager for the Advocacy division of The Recording Academy in Washington, DC (2013-2016).

OVERVIEW

Though I interviewed and wrote about hundreds of artists over my career, and certainly championed a few, I don't know that I had a hand in making anyone a star. Over the years people have thanked me for writing about them but, honestly, it's all a blur. Writing multiple stories, a week or a day, it's hard to remember individual stories. I did learn that sometimes writing a negative story or review had just as much impact, or more, than a positive one.

I do feel disrespected when I see stories about artists that use articles and headlines I wrote, but don't credit me or ask me to comment on camera. Looking back, I think I did good work, but I am not counted among serious music journalists from that time. It does make me angry to see numerous other women erased or overlooked in the history of our music, knowing all the hard work they put in often behind the scenes—behind the mic, as it were.

I am extremely thankful for the great women I connected with in my journey. Their support and advice made the huge difference for me.

Currently, I am a freelance writer and media & editorial consultant, providing writing, proofreading, editing, and publicity services as well as media training and book coaching services to business and individual clients under the Syllable Media LLC banner. I am also the creator and host of the *Words On Flicks* movie talk podcast.

Janine Coveney with Heavy D and the Boys, 1989

Mic Check 5

"Entertainment Is All Business"

~by~

LT Ladino

I am known in the industry as LT Clay/Bramble/Blassingame and though life changed my name several times while in the industry my love for being in entertainment never did. I'm proud to say I started out in the entertainment industry as a receptionist for the West Coast office of Jive Records in April of 1989. As I sat in my seat on the first day, I made a promise to myself that if in ten years I was not a Vice President, I would leave the industry. I never become a VP. Within nine years, I went from being a Senior Director at Columbia Records to a Senior Vice President of Marketing at Sony/Columbia//Loud Records.

I don't know that I ever had a chance to fall in love with music. It was something that was always a part of my life whether I loved it or not. I was born on Beethoven's birthday, in the 60s, in Detroit and had family members (my mother and uncles) who were performers. At first, I had no interest of going into the music industry... I wanted to be a doctor, i.e. heart or brain surgeon. I even took an accelerated science class as a child where we dissected cow hearts and brains at 11-years-old. But my mother preferred that would I follow her into the entertainment industry as a performer.

My mother's perspective was well intended since I grew up as a music industry brat. You see my mother was a background dancer and singer for James Brown and toured all over the world with his band from about 1970-1974 when I was a young child. All I've ever known was show business and I had an extended family of performers such as Al Green, The Commodores, The Chi-Lites, Maceo Parker, Fred Wesley and the whole James Brown Band, Dennis Edwards and Melvin Franklin from The Temptations, and so many more. Those in the industry knew my brother and me as "The Kitty Kats" or "Lupe's Kids" and we knew some of the most talented performers as Auntie or Uncle. Music was my everything and hanging out at The Apollo or Madison Square Garden on the weekends was the norm in my household.

Being a child birthed from Soul who ran to Rock music, I wasn't really into Hip Hop until I turned 19. Sure, I was familiar with Sugar Hill Records and the stylings of Kurtis Blow, Grandmaster Flash and the Furious Five and other Hip Hop records that made it on a popular station called KDAY in Los Angeles, but I was never exposed to it until my fiancé at the time took me to my first Hip Hop concert in Los Angeles. The concert featured Whodini, LL Cool J, Run DMC, and The Beastie Boys and I loved it. Here was this white boy exposing me to popular and underground hip hop like NWA, who knew all the words and dragged me to see underground performances all over Los Angeles.

I worked for years as an administrative assistant for several companies in the Los Angeles area including *The Hollywood Reporter* and *Advertising Age*. However, my goal was to wind up in the music industry. I never wanted to use the relations I had with those who worked for MCA or Sony Music. I wanted to find a job, learn the business and secure a role in the industry on my own. I was only able to do so by learning how to be a great administrative assistant with the ability to have strong follow-up skills, and the ability to befriend and manage all types of personalities. These two qualities were the building blocks for my growing into working in significant roles within the music industry.

I believe my greatest strength was my ability to be completely honest with the artists, managers, and colleagues I worked with. It would often get me into trouble but eventually, I became respected because I always saw things from a 360-degree view and had the ability to think of how a situation would affect everyone involved.

During my career, I have had the pleasure of working in the capacity of a Radio Promotions Manager and Publicist at Jive Records having worked with: BDP, KRS-One, D-Nice, Kool Moe Dee, Too Short, A Tribe Called Quest, Spice One, E-40, Souls of Mischief, Casual, Keith Murray, Fu-Schnickens, DJ Jazzy Jeff & The Fresh Prince, R. Kelly, Hi-Five, Angela Bofill, Billy Ocean, Aaliyah, Mystical.

As Product Manager at Arista Records & Columbia Records I worked with: Notorious B. I. G. OutKast, Goodie M.O.B., Monica, Usher, Dionne Warwick, Aretha Franklin, Mase, P. Diddy, John Forte, Pras, Maxwell, Lord Tariq & Peter Gunz, Stevie J, For Real, Donell Jones, Society of Soul, Fishbone, and Blaque.

As SVP of Marketing, I helped develop and brand projects for Wu-Tang Clan, Raekwon The Chef, Three 6 Mafia, Big Pun, Tha Alkaholiks, Xzibit, Mobb Deep, MOP, and LV.

We all know about the "IT" factor but the artists who were diligent in their craft and stay consistent with their branding were the true superstars. A hit record and instant success are fleeting. True talent is based on an artist's ability to understand what they want to accomplish in their career. R. Kelly was a great example of this. (Please note I do not condone the behavior that lead to Robert's arrest and conviction but the following is an account of his music and the brand awareness he shared with me back in 1993.) While working on the track "Summer Bunnies", for his 12 Play album, he told me that he wanted to have such a deep connection with his core fan base that it wouldn't matter what the first single would be it would be an automatic hit. I thought he was crazy and laughed at him. But think about it, he went on to release "You Remind Me Of Something", "Half On A Baby", "Feelin On Your Booty", and many others. To his genius, they all were smash hits and propelled him further into stardom. His musical talents weren't limited to R&B or soul. I have seen him do an ode to his mother one second, switch to an operatic intro for "Bump And Grind," and he talked about always having a strong affinity for wanting to write country music.

I have had several artists I took on as my pet projects. I loved working with those under 18-years-old. Having been around music from such a young age I felt it was my responsibility to help guide their careers. Artists such as Aaliyah, Usher, Monica, and Kimberly Scott will always hold a dear place in my heart.

Too Short was the most professional artist I ever worked with. When I met him in 1989, I immediately had an attitude because I told him I was not a Bitch. He explained that he had two personalities: Professionally, Too Short was the shit-talking, drinking, street hustler that everyone knows someone like him, and Todd Shaw was the person. I admired the way he was able to compartmentalize these personas and found him to be the nicest guy. Whenever he had a project out, Todd would often drive down from Oakland to Los Angeles, give me a call, take me out to lunch, and we would ride around in his whip stopping at mom-and-pop record stores for impromptu visits to talk with the owners and staff members. He was a class act all the way.

A Tribe Called Quest where my babies and were very dear to my heart and 100% genius. I remember meeting Q-Tip when he was about 18 or 19 in the Jive Records office when I was the receptionist who sat out front before this first album was released. He was quiet and sat listening to his Walkman rapping along with the tracks he played very expressively. When I was able to catch his attention, I asked what he was listening to. He looked at me blankly and said "Nothing." Puzzled I went over to him, and he showed me an empty cassette holder. Everything he heard was in his head and I believe I witnessed the process and the beginning of Q-Tip's brilliance as an MC that day.

Yet, the one project I felt I had much success with was R. Kelly. As the West Coast Regional Promotions/Media Relations Manager, it was my job was to get all music for Jive Records on the radio, mix-shows, and underground music scene. R. Kelly was the most commercial project Jive Records had on the roster since leaving a longstanding relationship with RCA. As my first major position in the industry, I was always looked upon as "The Baby" and felt I wasn't taken seriously by other promotions reps. Not to mention, with the least amount of radio outlets in my territory for urban music, I had less than ten stations in my region. There was a terrible rivalry with Aaron Hall because he felt R. Kelly stole his musical stylings but let's face it they both stole it from Charlie Wilson. Even though R. Kelly had experienced success all over the rest of the country the west coast wouldn't budge.

Doors continually were shut in my face trying to get my artist played. *The Arsenio Hall Show* refused to book him no matter how far he shot up the charts; to this day I'm convinced he was boxed out due to Aaron's friendship with Arsenio. Program Directors would lie to my face about adding R. Kelly's records and other label reps would talk badly about my artist. I had to make a few drastic moves to earn the respect of my peers. I could no longer be the meek rep I was but had to exert strength by cussing and flipping out at a Music Director at The Beat for taking advantage of me and another artist. I will always claim that I had nothing to do with two of my best friends falling in love with two of my music directors in my territory, but I was able to parlay those relationships to my advantage.

The most frustrating thing about working with R. Kelly was that people didn't see his talent right away. He never performed on *The Arsenio Hall Show* but I was able to book him on The Tonight Show with Jay Leno and he made his first late-night musical appearance performing "Bump and Grind" from his second album release.

The most frustrating thing about my job was all of the BS I had to put up with as a woman in the industry. I hated working on the guise of being a part of a "Black Music Department." I grew up with a variety of musical tastes and didn't like being hindered by just working Urban Music. The disrespect and cattiness women showed each other in the industry was also a problem for me.

Some of the challenges I faced as a woman in the industry were being belittled and not taken seriously, being challenged to disregard my morals for the sake of a project. Yet, my biggest challenge was not being mentored by a woman in the industry. I overcame those challenges by only standing up for myself and other women too. I've always had a voice and challenged the BS within the industry. I got in trouble at times because I refused to be taken as a fool. Regarding not having a female mentor, I decided to become one instead and helped several young female executives blossom and grow within entertainment.

My two favorite mentors were my VP of Artist Development at Arista Records, Richard Sanders, and my first boss former NARAS President Neil Portnow. I considered consider both to be like fathers and it is under their tutelage I have grown to be the executive I am today. Both offered sound advice and provided the tough love many of us need on occasion. With regards to my colleagues, I had a host of Sista friends who I could rely on for wise counsel like Sheri (Huguely) Riley, Tashion Macon, LaJoyce Hunter Brookshire, and Pamela Crockett.

Yet through it all I never wanted to quit throughout my career. I was raised to believe there is no such thing as quitting until the road changed and that didn't come until I actually did resign to focus on being a wife and mother to my two young sons in 2000. I became burned out and the industry was no longer fun for me. That's when I knew I needed a change.

Today my heart is delighted when I hear a track that I was assigned to back in the day being used in pop culture today. Like Gatorade using "93 Til Infinity" by Souls of Mischief in a commercial music bed or when a hardcore underground track like "Ante Up" by MOP received minimal radio airplay but is regularly used for commercials and movie trailers to a level of cool factor to a very mainstream product.

There is a great sense of pride that is unexplainable when I see my artists today still thriving and their music being exposed to a new generation decades after their release. It brings me joy and a floodgate of memories. When I hear those songs on the radio, I feel blessed to have shared that moment of space and time with them.

I cannot point to one moment as a greatest accomplishment as a mother shouldn't favor one child over the other. I count my experience as a whole as one of my greatest accomplishments in the 50 years I've been on this earth.

My most embarrassing moment was when I fought one of my artist's shows. We were in a packed club with no room to stand and a female patron became mad because as the record company representative, I wouldn't let her stand in the DJ booth with the VIPs I bought to the show. When I came out of the booth, she looked me in the eyes and intentionally poured her glass of red wine all over my new expensive velvet bustier top and said "Oops!" I lost it, my boxing lessons kicked in, and let loose a one-of-a-kind genuine ass whipping. It was her blatant disrespect of me that made me see red. She was kicked out and I had to compose myself and continue entertaining the VIPs who were with me and saw the whole thing. Making matters worse, the artist learned about the incident in disbelief as I rode in the limo with broken fingernails and a stained top. My bosses found out and it had gotten back to all of the regional record representatives in Los Angeles. Boy, did they tease me when they saw me that week. I never meant to make such a fool of myself, disrespect my company and regret my actions.

The one aspect of the job I loved most was the ability to discover new music before the marketplace. There was something exciting about receiving an advance copy of a single or album and being able to share that music with the marketplace.

My realization that I was a bona-fide ROCKSTAR behind the Mic was the moment I was with Monica at the Apollo. As she performed on stage, and I waited in the wings I was able to look out at the two seats in the fourth row that my brother and I sat every time we had to see our mother, or "Uncle and Auntie" perform when we were children. It was as if my life had come full circle and I knew I was right where I was supposed to be… in the music industry.

When I see biopics being made that have glaringly left out my fellow Women Behind The Mic sisters it pisses me off. Half of the time you see people that you never knew, and you are like "Who the heck is that?" or "Why are they interviewing them and not so and so?"

The one bit of advice I would share with young women about how to navigate the record/radio industry today is: Never shit where you eat. Keep your love life and your business separate. This way no one will be able to say that you slept your way to the top. It was something I stood on. For all of those who hit on me back in the day, they could *never* say they had me.

I left the industry because I became burnt out by the greed or illegal actions of many and wanted to focus on being a wife and mother. So much of my time was poured into my career. I began to feel the moments I lost and will never get back with my sons. I feel that in the early years the nannies were able to experience all of the milestones that I missed, and it took a while for me to forgive myself.

I gained a plethora of skills from the entertainment industry that aided in my ability to run my own entertainment marketing firm for many years. I was able to assist a clothing client who was not able to compete with Sean Jean or RocaWear because they couldn't afford to sponsor a credible music celebrity to represent their clothing line.

By using my overall marketing skills as a Product Manager, I was able to create a 30-market promotional retail campaign with over 300 Mom and Pop clothing stores to support the movie release of 8 Mile at a time when Editor-In-Chief Benzo at The Source Magazine vowed to ruin Eminem's career. Universal Pictures was concerned that they had a stellar film but were not able to get the support of urban audiences. So, I partnered the movie studio with my fashion client, Davoucci, replacing a series of their advertisements with an "Enter to Win" Sweepstakes to the screening. By doing so Davoucci was able to connect their brand with the iconic imagery of Eminem writing rhyme on his hand. Davoucci was an outerwear and sports line whose largest market was Detroit. The clothing line experience a 170% increase in sales in the 4th quarter when the film came out and Papa Doc is wearing a Davoucci shirt in the last battle scene in the film.

The greatest lesson from my career in music was that I learned how to manage people's expectations which was an art that needed to be mastered in the industry. I learned to always look for the business aspect of a venture and nurture it. The entertainment industry is a business and most fail to learn the business aspect of the music industry the same as if you were going to med school or law school.

If I had the chance I would tell my younger self this one piece of advice which is something I learned the hard way. First, be open but extremely shrewd when forming alliances in the entertainment business. Second, know that everyone doesn't have your work ethic. People will disappoint you based on the crabs in a barrel mentality; however, you will have the best time of your life so enjoy the ride.

What I miss the most about the industry is the camaraderie of being on a team with one common goal, helping artists turn their musical dreams into reality and sometimes the lifestyle.

My deepest regret is never being able to apologize to Biggie. I had just had my first son Caleb and traveled back to Los Angeles to show off my newborn to family and friends. This was the weekend of the Soul Train Music Awards show in 1997. I received a call from Bad Boy Records GM, Jef Burroughs, and Biggie's manager, Mark Pitts, that Biggie decided to blow off his international promo tour Arista the day he was supposed to fly out to stay in LA for the award show and its festivities. I cussed out Pitts and threatened to get the company to stop working on the new single "Hypnotize" and all of his artists if he didn't get Biggie on the plane.

I then called Biggie me and I cursed him with every colorful explicative I could think of regarding his size and skin color, and told him the same thing hoping it would get him on the plane. It didn't work. Biggie wasn't mad at me and he told me "Ma, I just wanted to party." I was so furious that I hung up on him. After the Soul Train Awards, I received a call at 3:30 am from Terri Haskins, Bad Boy's VP of Marketing, and my former colleague at Jive Records, that Biggie was dead. I was quiet because I didn't believe her. I just assumed it was another great Bad Boy marketing ploy. "I get it… That's brilliant. Biggie's album is called Life After Death so if you guys are spreading rumors that Biggie is dead then he can come out of nowhere and promote the album. Awesome plan."

She laughed nervously and said, "No, he is really dead!" My cellphone started blowing up and it didn't seem real until calls started to roll in with reports of Biggie's demise. I cried for hours feeling horrible about the last conversation I had with him and even today, I regret never having the chance to say sorry to one of my favorite rap artist.

I tried going back into the industry several times but the dynamic of what it was and what it has become is completely different than that of the glory days of the 90s. Though there are many successful artists out today, in my opinion they are not as talented as the artists I had the chance to work with or be around back in the day.

After deciding to leave the entertainment industry fully, I was led into the human capital industry as an executive recruiting professional. It has been over ten years and today, I am a career expert known as "The Employment Therapist™" having helped place hundreds and counseled thousands in perfecting their presentation and interviewing skills. I have taken the artist development skills that I learned from the music industry, and all of my "Slumdog Millionaire" experiences and created an HR Tech platform called vCandidates.com where I serve as CEO and Chairman of the Board. vCandidates.com helps job seekers become "viable candidates" with better career development tools. I am a published author and my suspense novel, *To And Fro: Kelsey's Journey* has been published on the Renewing Your Mind Ink and Peace In The Storm Publishing imprints.

LT Ladino with Aaliyah and BMG Distribution Staff

Mic Check 6

"Fair is My Weapon"

~by~

Crystal Whaley

I can't ever remember a time when I wasn't in love with music— "From the Cradle to the Grave", music lifts me and allows my soul to soar. Music was pivotal in my house. Everything revolved around music. My first official concert was going with my young parents as a toddler to the WattStaxx Concert by Stax Records at the Coliseum in Los Angeles the summer of 1972.

The first Hip Hop song I fell in love with "Good Times" (which I considered Hip Hop) by Chic that morphed into Sugar Hill Gang's "Rapper's Delight" and "Trans-Europe Express" by Kraftwerk.

I am a Howard University alum with a BA in Journalism as well as a Film Production/Producer certificate from New York University.

While in my first job at Uptown Records as a Promotions assistant in 1993 to James 'Jimmy Luv' Jenkins, I discovered video from the urgings of my film friends, director Hype Williams and his uber talented director of photography Malik Sayeed who were trying to break into music video production at the time. Being a Journalism major, telling stories always spoke to me, so I started to pay more attention to video.

I had a production company with director Alan Ferguson called Free Spirit Films in 1998.

I was a freelance Video Commissioner for various labels in Los Angeles & New York City from 2000-2002 and then again in 2004-2005. I was Director of Video Production for Arista Records from 2002–2004.

My greatest strength was simply being present, as a young woman Hip Hop Video Producer in that particular machismo system, I demanded respect for myself and running a respectful set spoke volumes during that time.

Throughout my career, producing music videos or commissioning, I worked with Biggie, Jay Z, Puff, 112, Mary J Blige, Big Bub, Res, Bilal, Common, Mobb Deep, OutKast, Usher, John Legend, Chris Brown, Snoop, Musiq Soul Child, Sunshine Anderson, Anthony Hamilton, Clipse, Bone Crusher, Lil Jon, Field Mob, Yin Yang Twins, YoungBloodZ, Ciara, Kelis, Dido, Pink, Sarah McLachlan, Avril Lavigne, Santana to name a few.

I could tell you which artists were going to be superstars by the track and hook of the song. I was lucky enough to be a part of a winning team at Arista that made videos a priority ensuring groundbreaking sales for Usher and OutKast.

I knew OutKast had the "IT" factor because of the risks they took creatively. This along with their signature production and lyrical prowess shut everyone and everything down. It really was their confidence, stage presence and being 'out of the box' that made them platinum artists.

One of my pet peeves when working with production companies directing multi-platinum artists, was (at times) their inability to stay on budget. I was a no 'overage' type of commissioner. The most frustrating thing about being a music Video Producer was last minute changes by either the director or the label that would affect my budget.

The most frustrating thing about being a music Video Commissioner was when the artists themselves, their entourages, their 'guests' made it a challenge for production by way of delays due to the shenanigans of the artists, which would result in overages. The other frustration was when a director didn't stay the course of the approved and commissioned video treatment and I would have to direct and edit to make our deliverables. This was rare, but it did happen.

While working as a female music video producer I've encountered and have dealt with some sticky situations where the environment was toxic and at times dangerous for my talent and crew. The challenges were demanding respect and taking my lead in a tricky situation not necessarily by the crew, but absolutely with artists and their 'crews'. We were all so young in our mid-20s, and I also looked extremely young. At first sight folks did not know the deal and many made attempts to try me which never served them or the production well.

I was able to overcome challenges because I always set a tone on my sets especially when I produced hard-core Hip Hop. Communication and simply being courteous and fair were my weapons. People respond better when you are clear, direct and courteous - even the hardest of the hard-core. Giving folks a visual, a picture of respect in myself and the way that I moved on set, was better that ever having to open my mouth.

My mentor in the industry was Connie Orlando who taught me how to produce music videos. I produced my first video The 112 Remix of "Only You" featuring Biggie through her production company. My champions were my young sister circle that included trailblazing Hip Hop journalists (many of them were the only or the first woman editor at critically acclaimed magazines), sisters in other industries who were also firsts and brilliant, along with all of my girlfriends working at labels became reflections of how to be and how to soar. We were a support system for each other.

To jump headfirst into production, I quit Uptown Records before I made a year, and have never looked back. The one thing that makes my heart sing is when OutKast sold over 20 million copies of *SpeakerBox/ The Love Below* album knowing it was the visuals for that album that took it over the top.

My greatest accomplishment was convincing Atlantic Records to let us shoot Big Bub's remake of the Commodores' classic "Zoom" in Dakar Senegal West Africa. We brought most of our crew, talent, and label. That was epic and we came in under budget!

My most embarrassing moment was while freelance commissioning for MCA Records and my artist would not come out of her trailer the entire day which made production lose the day.

As a Commissioner I loved steering the artist to the right Director to achieve the best product and ultimately awarding the job to the perfect Director for the project. As a music Video Producer, I loved working with my talented friends and making magic happen that ultimately are now classic videos and still stand the test of time. I am very proud to see the artists I work with still relevant today. It feels good to hear their music and it brings back memories from the most fantastic to the most ridiculous.

When I see Biopics being made who have glaringly left out The Women Behind The Mic, unfortunately it doesn't surprise me. I call it invisibility politics. It has tempted me to think about creating content highlighting all of us.

I would tell my younger self to be sure to maintain and sustain all of your relationships and to remain visible and open to all opportunities. My advice to young women navigating the record/radio industry today is to believe in yourself always. Be persistent. Carry a win-win attitude and gangster your 'follow through' game. Surround yourself with community that lifts and encourage you. Set standards at the beginning so that there is never a question of integrity and respect. Be clear, decisive and remain open to opportunities while you engage in self-care. Be fearless and ready to soar!

I have technically left music but not film. I often still work with talent and crew that worked with me as a video producer and as a commissioner, we've simply evolved in other newer spaces to tell our stories. What I miss the most about the industry is the camaraderie, the playfulness and the innocence. We had a good time. My deepest regret is not staying at a label longer than a year and a half. And not stepping up to direct when I had an opportunity. If I could work in the industry again, I would only enter as a consultant if the situation is right.

These days I am a bi-coastal multiple Emmy Award winning TV/ Film Producer, writer and finally a Director, still creating magic.

Mic Check 7

"Guard Your Reputation"

~by~

Dedra N. Tate

I grew up in theater. My sister and I both studied at Dance Theater Harlem and were also members of Junior Company Artistic Director Marie Brooks' Pan-Caribbean Dance Troupe, and later the Harlem Children's Theater Company. We performed at the Kennedy Center in Washington, DC and travelled extensively throughout the U.S. and the Caribbean, performing, and learning different styles of dance. My specialties were tap and ethnic dance...I guess I have always been into entertainment.

As a child, my home was always filled with music. I would to listen to every record, read every credit on the album covers, and write down every single lyric to my favorite songs in my Composition notebooks. I would play the record, pause it, write down the lyrics, and then sing it over and over.

During my high school years, my sister and I had a column in the *Amsterdam News*, New York's largest and most influential Black weekly newspaper. It was called "Tomorrow's Generation" by Jeanine & Dedra N. Tate. We went to every concert for free and interviewed everybody that was anybody. We travelled in limos and always had backstage passes. I always had that passion for music, even back then.

I really fell in love with music when the Jackson 5 came out. There were songs before them, and artists that I liked, who were mostly older, but when the Jackson 5 came out I was in heaven. Michael Jackson even called us on our home phone so we could interview him!

I started my career in entertainment at MTV Networks in 1984 as a Sales Assistant. I wanted to work there since I was a student at Howard University. My major was broadcast journalism and, at the time, I wanted to become the first Black Barbara Walters on television in front of a camera. When MTV launched and I saw they had Music News, I knew that was the place for me. I wanted to work there and I targeted that company.

Honestly, my whole career started due to nepotism. My father, Robert A. Tate Jr., has a huge personality, is extremely well- known, and loved by all. He's also a Howard grad and had a successful career as a marketing and advertising executive. He eventually left the corporate world and published three magazines. Throughout his career, he mentored dozens of young men and women, who had gone on to make their own marks in the business. When I asked if he knew anyone at MTV, he immediately put me in touch with one of his mentees who was an account executive there. That's how I got my foot in the door.

When I first started, I was a Sales Assistant and working at MTV was a dream come true. I fell in love with what they were doing in the Talent Relations Department, because they had the relationships with all of the record labels. They also were responsible for adding the videos and booking the celebs on the network. In sales, if we needed tickets to schmooze a client we would have to contact talent relations, and I knew, *That's where I want to be.* Within just a year, I was hired by the Vice President of Talent Relations, who became my first mentor, and I began working in my dream department.

While working at MTV during its heyday, I was surprised to see that most of the Black employees there were working in administrative positions, with the bulk of them in the accounting department. Even in the Sales department there were only two Blacks in a team of over thirty. I remember many of my peers telling me that I would never get the position in Talent Relations, when it was posted internally. During those years, there weren't even a handful of Black people working in the creative departments. I knew I had to have a carefully crafted plan of action and put it into motion! Not only did I parlay with the head of human resources to request the very first interview for the position, I did my research on my boss and knew he commuted from Long Island to the city for work. At the end of my interview, I told him "If there's anything I didn't cover, I know you commute so here's a little something for you to read on the train," and I presented him with a book I made for him, titled ***Dedra N. Tate & Why!***

My greatest area of strength has always been my communication and people skills. I call myself *the ultimate networker*, however, I am also a very private and protective person when it comes to my reputation and credibility. In this business, you must make sure that you treat people the way that you want to be treated. It's also very important to guard your reputation. I believe those are much needed personality traits, especially for women coming up in the music industry.

After three years at MTV, my boss called me in to his office to tell me he was leaving to start a record label with Elton John called UNI Records. He wanted to take me with him, but had a non-compete clause in his contract. He set up a meeting with the President of MTV and asked him what the plans were for promoting me in the talent relations department to a higher position, because he had an immediate opportunity for me to grow. If they didn't have something that was comparable, he asked if they would release him from the non-compete clause so that he could take me with him. The company allowed it and that's how I segued from MTV to the record label side of the industry.

I have been very lucky to have mentors, throughout my career, who were great leaders, respectful and never had me deal with sexual harassment. I've always been surrounded by professional men who have really helped me make sound decisions and gave me amazing opportunities.

At UNI Records, I worked in the Promotions, the department that is responsible for getting the records played on the radio. Also, back then, we didn't have a retail team so I would also go in and set-up record store displays for artist appearances. I started out as a National Promotions Coordinator, so I supported our team members across the country. We would have to take our artists to all of the radio stations and record stores, to do what they called "in-stores." Because our team was small, I was able to get a 360-degree experience, between radio stations, record stores and video shoots. Performances were during the evenings and we would host meet-n-greets for the fans and our radio and retail contacts to maximize exposure for our artist in each marketplace.

Now, this is what I loved about my era of the music industry. Back then, when you were a promotions person, getting your records played, and even getting in to meet with the program director at the radio stations, relied on the strength of your personal relationships. This is an area that I excelled in, and it goes back to my morals and reputation. It was important that you carried yourself with respect, were responsible, personable, and likable. Those qualities helped me to open doors, and playlists, for my artists. Every station has a "radio day" once a week, where the promotions person from every record label sits in the station lobby waiting for their turn to see the Music Director. I was always able to go into each of my stations, take the Program Director completely out of the building, for lunch, and even bowling, while I talked about my artists and that's how I got my records added.

Today, it is different. Program Directors base everything on spins and followers, so it's a little more cut-and-dry. These days, their relationship with the promotion person carries little weight and the focus is primarily on data and research. They took the personality out of promotions, which was a personality game.

My career has been a beautiful continuous flow of movement that transitioned me from one company to another, seamlessly. All of my positions have been like connect the dots, from MTV to UNI to MCA to Motown to Flavor Unit.

At UNI I promoted Fine Young Cannibals hit song "She Drives Me Crazy" and we also had a British group named Transvision Vamp on our label.

UNI was mostly European and real Pop music. Then, out of the blue, my boss announced that we just signed a deal with Strong City Records, a Hip Hop label, and also did a one off-deal with Def Jam Management's Lyor Cohen for Eric B and Rakim's *Follow the Leader* album. Lucky for me I inherited both of these projects. I was the only Black person working at Uni and they were my babies.

The first Hip Hop song I fell in love with was "Rapper's Delight," and now I was working with my first Hip Hop group, which was Eric B. & Rakim. I was already a huge fan, and we released their hits "Follow the Leader" and "Microphone Fiend," to name a few. I was living and breathing Hip Hop and loved traveling to the R&B music conventions, like Jack the Rapper and Impact, with my artists.

One day, I ended up getting on the elevator with Jheryl Busby, the President & CEO of MCA Records, because UNI was on the same floor as their NY offices. When I told him where I worked, he said, "Really, I thought only White people worked there." I jokingly said, "That's why I call it Uni, because I'm the only Black person here." We both fell out laughing.

Jheryl soon became my mentor and he stayed in touch with me when he went back to LA. As soon as a position became available at MCA, he told his team, "I want Dedra Tate hired." I actually had the job before the company even listed the position as available. At MCA's New Edition Album Release and Christmas Party, Jheryl announced that I was the new Northeast Regional Promotion Manager at MCA.

Throughout my career I have worked with New Edition, Stephanie Mills, Boyz II Men, Another Bad Creation, Johnny Gill, Bobby Brown The Good Girls and Queen Latifah, to name a few.

One of the things I used to do with our new artists is have them perform everywhere, and anywhere. If the flight was delayed, there was a free show. If we missed our bus, there was a free show. If we were killing time in the hotel lobby, there was a free show. I used to always run into artists who knew I was in the business, and they would say, "I'm a singer or a rapper." The first thing I would always say is, "Let me hear you."

The ones that choke up are the ones that weren't ready because they were stumbling and fumbling, they just weren't serious. I used to teach my artists to always be prepared and to be ready when someone asked them to show what they can do. That is rule number one in artist development.

When Jheryl gave Michael Bivins a production deal, we had a lot of artists who were minors. I would wonder, "*Will I ever get out of the world of finding, and hiring, tutors to go on the road with us?* Working with young acts was like being their "other" mother, but I loved it and developed special bonds with those artists. At Motown, my babies were Boyz II Men, Another Bad Creation (ABC), Subway and 702.

Being on the road with young children, and teenagers, was the extremely exciting. People who are in the business, that have never worked with young artists have missed out on a different level of experience. Kids are still kids in their daily lives. I can just imagine how it was with The Jackson 5. If you saw the mini-series, they were always playing pranks, hiding and people not being able to find them, not paying attention to their tutor, and them just being amazed and in awe of everything. They acted like they were not even the artist, but like they were the fan of every single person they were in the presence of. To me, it was such a rewarding experience because you didn't get that same feeling with a lot of the older artists, who may have been jaded, or were demanding. With the young kids, every single thing was an adventure. They keep you super young, high-spirited, and excited, because their excitement and openness to the music business was a brand-new and unbelievable world revealed to them.

Whenever my young artists were in town, I would have to round-up my nephew Robbie, my little cousins, and friends kids to entertain their behinds. I would do things with them that you would do with a young family member like take them to the movies, take them out to eat at fun places, or even cook for them at my house. Anything to get them out of that hotel environment, where they could get into a lot of trouble. That made it more personal as well. I actually did that with all of my artists. If my family was having a reunion, picnic or cookout, I would take them with me if they were in town. That's one of the things that all of my artists said they appreciated because I treated them more like family, instead of just like an artist. I would personally pick them up when it was time to go do something and also made sure that whenever they were in my town, or in my territory, that I created an entire itinerary that was full of work, and play.

Shortly after I started working at MCA, Jheryl decided to leave to take over the reins of Motown from Berry Gordy, and he took me with him. I was at Motown for a total of eight years, and during that time Jheryl gave Michael Bivins, from New Edition, his own label called Biv 10 Records. Jheryl and Michael named me general manager because of my great work relationships and success promoting Boyz II Men and Another Bad Creation, in my markets, when I worked with them at Motown.

While I was the general manager of Biv 10, Jheryl signed Queen Latifah and that's how I met her and her partner, Shakim Compere. They liked what we were doing with our artists at Biv 10, and asked me if I would be interested in coming to New Jersey to help them transition Flavor Unit from being a management company into an entertainment company.

During my 13-year tenure at Flavor Unit, the company grew from management to three record labels and then segued into TV and film production. *The VIBE Awards* was one of our first productions. We created it, from inception, as a joint-venture between Vib*e* Magazine, CBS, and Flavor Unit and I served as supervising producer for the three years we produced the show. I also started bringing in TV and film ideas and projects to Shakim. Eventually, I created my own company so that if Flavor Unit passed on a project I could still work on it without being in conflict. I even brought my director Jerry Lamothe to the company, He was the writer/director on the first film I produced, *Black Out*, starring Jeffrey Wright, Zoe Saldana and Michael B. Jordan. I wanted to sign Jerry to Flavor Unit management but Shakim was doing comedies, not dramas. That's when I asked if I could give Flavor Unit a first right of refusal, and still stay there while working on outside projects they passed on. That is how my company, Unlimited Contacts, Inc., was born.

Unlimited Contacts, Inc. was actually the name of my Dad's company, but when I was trying to think of a name for my company, that name just kept popping up. I guess you can say I inherited Unlimited

Contacts from him because his company was only registered in the state of New York, so that's how I was able to use the name as well. I eventually registered my company and was able to get my own Tax ID.

I could tell which artists were going to be superstars based on their natural talent, and also what kind of support they were going to get from their record label. Promotions reps are very familiar with each project because we sit in on the A&R meetings where they play new music to get our feedback. This is key because we are the ones that get the records played on the radio. From that point, you can tell, from the excitement of the team, who was going to be exceptional and get the support they need from the label. It's not who's got the most talent, it's who's got the hottest record. Whomever has a hit, that's who the company is going to put money and resources behind. If you don't have the support of the label, that means you're not a priority and the chances of being successful are slim. There can be someone more talented, or equally as talented, as someone else on the label, but if they had a manager that was closer with the head of A&R they may have been able to negotiate a bigger budget. An artists team can be a blessing, or a curse. If the label has a problem with an artists' manager, the entire project can be shut down and they will no longer be a priority, no matter how talented they were. I think a lot of human interaction can definitely block someone's road to super-stardom.

Hindering someone from their rise is a most unfortunate thing. I did have a situation like that with someone who was in a position I held, before me. They tried to sabotage me by taking the entire rolodex with all the radio contacts I needed to perform my job. I showed up on the first day of work, and things that should have been there were gone. I never understood why. I resented that person at first, but realized that I had to let it go because if you hold on to things from the past, you'll never be able to receive the blessings that are in store for you, I learned that you forgive and move on.

A very sad time in my career was when my mentor Jheryl Busby passed away. I have to say I have been blessed to have many other mentors who taught me valuable lessons. I admired and learned from Sylvia Rhone Linda Haynes and, of course, Michael Bivins. While working alongside Michael, I learned so much about the mastery of marketing and artist development. He was definitely a star-maker!

I loved my career and never felt like quitting. As a matter a fact, there were times that I needed to quit but I didn't know it. Before I knew it, I was 35 years old without a husband and had no children, because I was a workaholic. That's one thing that I know, God has a plan for everything. I didn't end up getting married until I was 35. My friends all had grown kids and I didn't want to quit, but I absolutely knew I had to pause and take some time to get this part of my life fixed.

I would often attend "couple's events," I would ponder, *I don't even have a person that I'm thinking about dating*. I didn't even have any time for a personal life and I never shut it down long enough to seriously date anyone. I would always say, "I'm busy," because I put work first for so many years. I started my career when I was 20 years old, and for 15 years I was going hard around the clock. It was not sustainable.

I have no regrets, but I think that everything happened in its own time. In hindsight, I may not have advanced as far, in my personal career, if I had a child when I was younger. At age 37, my son Jian was born and he had asthma. Luckily, and I was working at Flavor Unit during that time and had moved to New Jersey. I had a lot more flexibility, and travel was optional, so I was able to raise my son. That would not have been the case before. Back in the day, when my female colleagues were pregnant, it was like they were simply counting the days until they had to be back at work. It was crazy. I always say that of all of my decades in the entertainment industry, my greatest production is my son and my greatest joy is being his mother.

I didn't have a lot of the challenges many women have had in the industry. My situation was unique because, although I was a woman, I was always treated like one of the fellas. I was able to always play, hang, and go hard with any guy. I was always at the table, and always had a seat at the table.

I was always able to fit in, and have conversations with presidents and CEOs. They would even invite me to their homes for special events, and I still find this true today. I am invited into a lot of circles, and I think that's because it goes right back to personality and the personal relationships I've built with people over the years. I've also mentored countless young men and women in this business. Some of the women have had issues with men in this business being inappropriate. I have always been supportive of them and shared how they should handle certain situations.

No room was ever difficult to me. Some people just take their industry jobs, relationships and lifestyle way too seriously. I've seen many instances where people have lost their position, and everything that came with it, because they were superficial. You must be genuine and truthful. If you tell someone they can call you, when they do, you'd better answer.

I think one negative thing I've encountered is the same thing that a lot of women in Hollywood are going through, which is not being compensated the same rate as their male counterparts. During the latter part of my career is when I actually started getting percentages/royalties for my work. During my career, most people received a yearly bonus. I was fortunate to work for a company that also gave out discretionary bonuses. This was a check, usually presented in person, that was a "thank you" for your personal contribution to the success of the company. The amounts were significant and not everyone received them. To me it was similar to a profit sharing system. When I was at Motown, I was rewarded yearly. I was actually able to purchase my first condo in Manhattan from the bonuses Jheryl gave me. I also learned to always have a five year plan, work at different companies to negotiate, and understand, contracts. I have been blessed to work with amazing people who gave me major opportunities that advanced my career, like Jhery.

I thoroughly enjoyed *The New Edition Story*, but the thing that I had a big problem with was how they portrayed my mentor.

Jheryl was one of the most considerate, laid back, soft-spoken and supportive people that I've ever met and I felt like he was portrayed as some type of tough guy! I had to ask myself, *Who approved this script?!* I did love how they developed the backstory, with the group members starting out as kids in a talent show, and the struggle their families went though as they grew up in the projects of Boston. When they joined MCA, Louil Silas, who was the head of A&R, and Jheryl took them to a whole other level.

The first thing I would say to any young lady entering the industry today is to make sure you have a great support system before you even enter those waters. If you don't have a solid foundation, with people who genuinely love you and can constantly reality check you, I think you will only be able to tread the waters for a little while and then drown.

If I could give my younger self some advice, it would be to slow it down a tad, do more things for myself, and that would include having more of a personal life, way before the age of 35.

To date, I have been able to successfully maintain my company, Unlimited Contacts, Inc. doing all the things I've grown to love in the entertainment industry. I still manage artists, work with producers, produce films and I'm still hosting and producing events! Actually, all of us were mini event planners, in our own right. Whenever an artist was in our market, we made it happen! We put together the parties, we got the DJs, and anything else that was needed. All of those skills are utilized underneath my Unlimited Contacts Inc. banner, in addition to public speaking engagements and mentoring.

I also currently serve as the Executive Producer & Director of Event Production for Black Health Matters—the leading health, wellness and chronic disease interactive digital platform dedicated to improving health outcomes among African Americans. We produce large, and small-scale, live, hybrid and virtual events, podcasts and webinars. I also produce events for The Whole Woman and pen a lifestyle and entertainment column, in the *New York Beacon* newspaper, titled #HotOffThePress.

Dedra N. Tate with Bel Biv DeVoe and Brook Payne

Mic Check 8

"Do Your Job"

~by~

Audrey LaCatis

I grew up in Detroit, one of the great music cities. I lived in the same neighborhood and went to school with the kids of many Motown artists and producers (which later made me realize Motown wasn't paying their people because I did not grow up in a rich neighborhood). We had a very in a musical household, my mother was a singer, but had to quit singing to get a better paying job to help support our family. My parents loved music of all genres We had hundreds of records of classical, jazz, blues, Broadway, funk, rock, pretty much everything except country. As children, my sisters and I played records all the time, every day.

I remember taking my allowance money to Monroe Records store and buying 45s. I loved The Ohio Players, Jackson 5, Led Zeppelin, Joni Mitchell, Al Green, and all the Motown acts as a pre-teen. In my high school years, I got way more into funk. My older sister's boyfriend played with George Clinton, and I remember going to the studio with

to: Audrey LaCatis
h Aretha Franklin

her and watching them record. It was magical. Rufus was big in our household. Marvin Gaye and Stevie Wonder were like gods to me. Still are. I went to junior high with Stevie's brother and sister. Music has always, ALWAYS, been a big part of my life. I became a Prince fan with his first album, as he got a lot of airplay in Detroit very early in his career.

The first Hip Hop songs that got me interested in Hip Hop were "Planet Rock", "It's Like That", and "The Message". I started really loving Hip Hop with Self Destruction, Eric B & Rakim, and I was obsessed with Big Daddy Kane (not just because he was fine AF, but his clever lyricism and use of metaphors); Public Enemy for their rawness and messages; Salt & Pepa were so much fun; MC Lyte, Doug E. Fresh, Slick Rick, EPMD—Hip Hop was amazing in the late 80s.

I moved to New York from Detroit, where I felt there were no opportunities for anything. I did not move there to pursue a career in music specifically, but I knew I wanted to do something that I would not have been able to do in Detroit. Once I arrived, as I completed my BA degree at The New School. I had to work through college to support myself, so I wasn't able to do free internships. My undergraduate work was in Communications, with a master's in international Affairs. I had taken Public Relations courses, learning how to create press plans, write releases, and how to pitch stories, but my training was not specific to the music business.

I worked as an assistant in the Ad Sales department at *Rolling Stone* magazine, which was how I started meeting people in the music business. I fell into the industry through contacts I made while working there. I wouldn't say there was a deliberate career path leading me to the industry as much as sheer luck and being able to take advantage of opportunities that were presented to me. I got involved in PR working with fledgling artists I met while at *Rolling Stone*.

My first 'real job' in the entertainment industry was as Director of R&B Publicity at Arista Records from 1990-1993. I learned a lot on the job, from my wonderful first boss, Melani Rogers, and from observing and following industry trends. The female label publicists were like family—I got a lot of help from many who started before I did. Many are still friends nearly 30 years later.

Arista wasn't a Hip Hop label, but we had Three Times Dope and some other acts that didn't break through. I liked Three Times Dope and they worked hard with the few press opportunities available at that time. At the end of my time at Arista, we finally started getting into the game with imprints like LaFace Records who signed TLC, and OutKast, and Dallas Austin's Rowdy. I wrote the very first Bad Boy press release but left Arista before any of the Bad Boy records were released.

In 1994, I moved to Atlanta to work with Dallas Austin, the founder of Rowdy Records - an imprint with Arista. I took the position because I really believed in his vision as a producer and artist. I only lasted six months in ATL. I absolutely *hated* living there and we were not putting out records. I was bored and frustrated. Luckily for me, a recruiter reached out to me about a job at Tommy Boy Records. I got the job and went back to NYC. I stayed at Tommy Boy three years from 1994-1997. At Tommy Boy, I worked with Naughty By Nature, De La Soul, Coolio, Capone & Noreaga, Big Noyd, many singles deals and EP releases as well. We put out a few hit soundtracks too—soundtracks were huge back then!

I segued into television production in 1998. I think my best work has been in the television production years of my career. My favorite job was on the *Chris Rock Show* on HBO, the first of three shows I've done with Chris. He has been amazing to me and is the best boss anyone could hope for. On the HBO show, we were able to book and produce music performances based on what we liked, rather than chart positions. He and I have similar taste in music, we like a variety of genres. We broke Jill Scott nationally as an artist, and Jay-Z did his first big TV appearances with us.

Others I got to book were OutKast, D'Angelo, Red Hot Chili Peppers. We were known for cool music, so much so, that when Sade put out her first album in ten years, she wanted to perform on Chris' show ahead of the big talk shows at the time like *The Tonight Show* and *Letterman*. The work on Chris' show led me to LA briefly to produce music segments for the Orlando Jones FX talk show and many other jobs over the years.

During my Arista years and working with Clive Davis, he always talked about star power. A lot of very talented singers tried to get signed to Arista, but he was adamant about singers needing "IT" - star power. When I started in television, I loved getting pitches for new artists and remembered my lessons from Mr. Davis and how to look for star power.

One of my favorite artists to work with was Aretha Franklin. When at Arista, she took me on as her main point of contact at the label, a tradition that she started with Tracey Jordan and Jackie Rhinehart before me, and LaJoyce Hunter Brookshire and Gwendolyn Quinn after I left. Working with her opened more doors than most artists can. I was proud to work to uphold her legacy.

I really loved Naughty by Nature. I started working with them after their massive hits "OPP" and "Hip Hop Hooray", and it was sad to see how MTV and the mainstream media turned their backs on them because they didn't have an anthem on their third album. So, I worked extra hard for them. Their work ethic was insane, and I loved that they took kids from their neighborhood out on the road with them to expose them to life outside East Orange, New Jersey. They uplifted a lot of people. The sustainability and legacy of Naughty By Nature has been wonderful to see unfold over the years. They still tour and their role in taking Hip Hop mainstream cannot be overstated. Many artists over the years that I was able to take a chance on early in their careers have become superstars. It was very satisfying to give new acts a shot and see them blow up later.

At the time when I did PR for Hip Hop acts, not getting 'mainstream' press to cover them was frustrating because we knew white kids were listening to Hip Hop and that it wasn't just 'a Black thing.' Even after Coolio was nominated for Record of the Year with "Gangsta's Paradise," the highest Grammy honor, and we couldn't get him a lot of covers. We got *Saturday Night Live* and a lot of TV, but I'll never forget the booker from *The Tonight Show* calling to ask, "Do you think he'll win the Grammy?" and of course I said, YES! That is the only way she considered booking him.

Every artist has behaviors that will drive their team crazy. But they wouldn't be stars if they were just like us, would they? Artists who were always late are the most frustrating.

I really hated when Radio Promotions departments couldn't get airplay on a dud record but expected us to get press on artist with no story. Infuriating!

As a woman working in the industry, it is hard to know where to start to outline the challenges. From all the misogynistic talk in meetings, the lyrics we had to promote, being hit on and having men try to feel you up, people mistaking you for a groupie when out with your artists, how many times I have been called a "Bitch," it became so normalized. I've been almost raped how many times? By male Executives…not artists. Really awful people.

I was able to overcome by reminding myself: Don't wear sexy outfits when out with artists. Avoid being alone in a room with most males. I was quite vocal when men made misogynistic comments, and luckily at Tommy Boy we had a female president (Monica Lynch), but we constantly had to listen to 'locker room banter'. I got teased for not wanting to go to the strip club with the fellas and the artists. I have quit jobs before. I don't believe in being miserable. Life is too short. Sometimes you reach a point when you know it's time to go. I had a lot of friends I could vent to. Tons. Almost all of them women, and almost all of them still friends today.

Some of my champions and mentors were Dedra Tate, Melani Rogers, and Jackie Rhinehart in early years of doing PR. The late great Lesley Pitts and Wendy Washington told me about the Chris Rock show job, and when I first submitted my resume, Nelson George told me the HBO execs thought I had too much music and not enough TV experience, so I resubmitted with a whole package on what I would do if I got the job. It worked. I'll always appreciate Nelson for that help.

Some stand out moments for me was every time Aretha would call my name from the stage was unbelievable. I loved every moment with her. Even when she was what some called difficult. I saw her as someone who had paid all the dues and deserved to have things her way. Also, the time Sade wanted to do the *Chris Rock Show* because she loved the music performances I booked and produced. Sade liked MY work!? I was DONE.

I don't really count accomplishments or claim anything, because everything I have ever done has involved a team. But I worked the hell out of that "Gangsta's Paradise" record, the *Bodyguard* soundtrack, and the *Boomerang* soundtrack was also huge in terms of press and radio hit. I made a lot of mistakes in early years as a publicist. Not putting my phone number on press releases, forgetting other pertinent info. Just dumb, careless mistakes that made me cringe when I caught them.

In PR work, I loved seeing a great article about an artist, but I always loved the TV performances the best. For Coolio's performance of "Gangsta' Paradise" at the *Billboard Awards*, we got Stevie Wonder to come out mid-song and sing his verses from "Pastime Paradise", which of course was the main sample on the song. I remember LA Reid looking over at me and saying, "You did that!" That was a moment.

The moment I knew I was doing a good job was during a long period of time at Arista when I had no department head and Clive Davis was being honored at the Friars Club. It was a huge star-studded event, and I had to lead on all the press coverage. At the end of the night, he gave me a heartfelt hug and thanked me profusely. He was very emotional about the night.

It is fantastic knowing I helped artists who are still relevant today along the way, and very gratifying. Hearing those songs, I worked on radio is nostalgic since I worked in music so long ago! But again, it's all teamwork. That is why stories are being told without the Women Behind The Mic I feel outrage. We're always left out.

The one bit of advice I would share about success in this industry came from Miller London, a veteran label executive. He told me many years ago that the key to success in the music biz or any industry is simple. DO YOUR JOB. Meaning don't get caught up in politics, gossip, and the rah-rah. Do your job. Stay focused and you'll be fine. I probably should have listened to that advice more because it is harder than it sounds.

The advice I'd give to my younger self is to not let my emotions get in the way of my job. I did that too often. Passion can lead to emotional decisions, and I could have done a better job of managing that. Biggest regrets: Not taking better care of myself. Putting my career ahead of my personal life.

I'm happy that I worked in the music industry during a time when we had fun, there was camaraderie, we traveled, we had conventions, we worked music that was really ground-breaking in the 90s. What I miss most were the expense accounts! And the family camaraderie—we were all family.

I wouldn't want to work as a publicist now, nor on the types of television shows I did in the past. I had a great time, but it was time to pass the torch. It is OK to check the rear view mirror once in a while, but I prefer looking forward.

The skills I gained in the entertainment industry have been writing, project management, logistics, diplomacy, budget planning which have all been transferable skills.

In the past five years or so, I have moved into the non-profit space and recently launched a Speaker Talent Agency with two phenomenal women I've worked with over the years. I'm not completely out of the entertainment business, since I work with celebrity talent for speaking engagements, corporate events, and private concerts. I love remote work now and can travel more, and work from anywhere!

I am also practicing more self-care than I ever have before and am happy. Life is beautiful.

Audrey LaCatis with Coolio and Stevie Wonder

Mic Check 9

"Trust Yourself and GO!"

~by~

Verna M. Miles

Ever since I can remember I have been in love with music! I come from a family who is musically inclined—singing in church, living the Hip Hop life. When I was little I heard my family harmonizing Gospel songs A Capella in the kitchen. Next it was the Jackson 5. Then when I heard my first Rap song, it was over! The first Hip Hop song I fell in love with was "Rapper's Delight" by The Sugar Hill Gang.

Growing up, music was everything to me. I escaped from everything and anything to music. No matter what I was going through music was always there for whatever mood I was in. I always added what I thought the song needed or told anyone who would listen, "What they should have done on this song is…"

I attended The High School of Fashion Industries in NYC at my parents urging because they felt I would have a more stable career. Years later I saw an artist named "Babyface" who changed my life. Although I had started a different path, I wanted to do everything that he did. So, I went to school to learn how to read and write music to be able to score films as well as write, produce, play, and sing. None of which I use now. I have attended Hofstra University and have a B.S. degree.

My career started as a Sony Music Intern in 1997. From 1998-2002 within the Sony system, I was a Marketing Coordinator/ Administrative Assistant, A&R Coordinator, A&R Manager and A&R Director with Tally Galbreth on the "Bulletproof Wallets" CD, Ghostface Killah.

My greatest strength I feel is that I am blessed by God to be a people person. I work well with artists and understand them as people first, talented second. I was also given the blessing of being able to spot talent and knowing a "Hit" when I hear one!

Some of the artists I have worked with have been Ghostface, Killah, Cappadonna, Cam'ron, Bone Thugs, Charlie Baltimore, Untertainment Records, B2K, Puerto Rock.

I could tell which artists were going to be stars by their passion! Talent only goes but so far, but passion, drive and dedication that is what makes stars.

My pet artist was Ghostface Killah. While he was incarcerated, he would call the label and I got to know him as a person and not just an artist. Once his project was released, we had a really good working relationship. Ghost knew who was real and who wasn't. He really did not like to deal with the "wasn't" which I respected, but it was challenging. I would say working with Ghost on his projects as well as handing as many things as I did successfully were my greatest accomplishments.

As A&R manager, I oversaw all A&R administration for the label along with such artists as B2K, 3LW, Jill Scott, Mandy Moore, Ghostface Killa, and Glen Lewis. Adding co-executive album producer to my credit for *A Season of Soul and Sounds of Christmas* album and A&R Director for the Ghostface Killah *Bulletproof Wallets* album. I organized and executed special projects for Epic Records that included the negotiation of production contracts and the processing of development and demo deals. Being the direct contact for all departments in the Epic Urban Group for business affairs and A&R administration has given me the ability to understand the artists' business needs while staying true to their aesthetic sense to be creative.

The most frustrating thing about my job was being a woman in the male dominated A&R department. My ideas were sometimes accepted but never credited, or my opinions taken, or if my ideas and opinions were accepted, they were used without any credit being given to me. Not having a voice at certain times in the midst of the whole "Boys Club" mentality definitely helped me to learn to trust my opinion and understand that I had great ideas. Fortunately, I could count on Susan Moultrie, Michelle Joyce, and Kelly Green for sound advice when challenges were front and center. These women had survived many changes and regimes and been successful in a male driven industry.

Yes, I felt like quitting hundreds of times but my mother taught me to never give up on a dream, and NEVER let anyone push you out of something that you know is your destiny! Besides the industry was so seductive. The release parties, never waiting in a line, the music, the artists, the perks!

One of my fondest memories was meeting Babyface at a Sony breakfast and having a one-on-one conversation with him. I was so overwhelmed I could hardly speak! The aspect I most enjoyed with my job was working directly with the artist, going to the studio for the creative process, and attending concerts with the artists.

I realized I was a Rock Star in the industry when I suggested to Ghost about putting out the song "Cherchez La Ghost" for women at his listening party and then the record was a success.

I am a believer that with God you can do anything! It feels great to see my artists doing well. When I hear the songs on the radio that I have Executive Produced like a Christmas album with an Epic artist I hear every year at Christmas time, and any of the Wu Tang records, bring back fond memories if being at 36 Chambers Street in New York City!

When I see Biopics and documentaries being made and leaving out all of the women, it hurts because I know the truth of how much we put into artists and their projects. We spent so many hours—seven days a week most of the time—just to make sure things were correct in whatever capacity we worked. We made sure the artists had what they needed, or they were in place where needed.

The biggest piece of advice I have is to listen and learn. Take what you've learned, trust yourself and go! Then relax, things are going to work out if you have tenacity. I left the industry because it was too much stress. My deepest regret is that I worked stressed most of the time. I didn't like the way things were going and I figured that I could do more on the other side of music starting an Indie (Independent) label. I gained a lot of amazing skills because I did so many things at Epic that I now have everything I need to run my own Indie label. I know every aspect of an artist's career and I am able to handle it all. I know how to work with my artists, and I understand the "business" of music.

The greatest lesson: Trust my instincts. If I think an artist has "It" or if I feel I have a hit song, trust that I do. Don't ever let anyone out-talk me or tell me what I should do with an artist. If I could give my younger self one piece of advice it would be...You know more that you think you do! Relax.

If given the opportunity I would not return to a company, I like what I am doing now more. Currently I am working with a Latina Girl Band on my Indie label.

Mic Check 10

"No One Moment"

~by~

Wendy Day

I started listening to Rap music in 1980 when I lived in Philadelphia. I love the energy and the passion in the music...and the truth in the music. In 1987, I went to New York City for a weekend with a friend and heard the Mr. Magic and Marley Marl radio show. Within two weeks, I quit my job, rented a U-haul, and moved to New York! I needed to be where radio shows like that were broadcast. I started in the Entertainment industry as a fan of Rap music.

My education didn't really prepare me for the music industry. I have an undergraduate degree in graphic design, I have a Master's degree in African-American studies, and I have an MBA in Marketing from McGill in Montreal. My background is sales and marketing, and I spent the first 30 years of my life trying to figure out what it is I wanted to do. I thought making money would have value to me because I grew up kind of poor, but money didn't make me happy. So, I stopped chasing money and decided to do what I love most. I decided I wanted to help empower people of color through entrepreneurship and help Rap artists—give back some of the happiness and support that their music brought me over the years as a Hip Hop fan.

But it wasn't until 1992 that I started Rap Coalition, a non-profit artist advocacy organization, to empower, unify, protect, and educate Rap artists, producers, and DJs—on the business side of the Music industry.

Rap Coalition is, and always has been a not-for-profit organization. Artists don't pay for our help. I own a for profit company called PowerMoves which has negotiated artists into exceptional ownership deals in the Urban Music industry (No Limit, Cash Money, etc.) and more importantly, taught artists how to put out their own music and make money with their music. I believe artists should retain ownership and I see the value in artists securing investors to fund their careers independently. This allows them to start their own labels and bring on other artists behind them that may not have the proper funding or access to investors or capital.

I don't think any education could prepare me for the music industry. But the #1 thing that qualified me to do what I do in music was running a small liquor company in Montreal in the late 1980s. Studying African American studies from an Afrocentric point of view taught me the importance of people of color owning their own companies and art form, and the MBA in Marketing taught me how to spread the music so artists could retain ownership while making the lion's share for the income from their own music. Even though Rap Coalition is a not-for-profit organization, my consulting company PowerMoves is for profit. However, I realized very early on in the music business that I would never become wealthy through music, because I was never willing to do what was necessary in order to get rich in the music industry. In order to become wealthy in music you must be willing to take ownership of an artist's publishing (the ownership of the actual music and words) and I was never willing to do that.

What really prepared me for the Urban Music industry was growing up to be comfortable as an outsider. My whole life I was always an outsider—the other. I grew up kinda poor in a wealthy neighborhood. My family was Christian in a Jewish neighborhood. I didn't have a strong sense of family or "tribe" (to quote a business a guru) because I was adopted and was always aware of that fact. And being that outsider prepared me to be at ease as a White female in a mostly male, African American dominated music industry.

What led me to entertainment was when I started selling advertising in magazines *Time* and *Sports Illustrated*. Then I moved to Canada from New York City and ran a liquor company in Montreal which gave me the balls to be entrepreneurial when I realized I could build a successful company myself. When I came back to the US in 1992, I got into the music industry by building my own company. I've never worked for a company since then. I was 30 years old. Most of my peers were in their early 20s at that time. There's that outsider thing again. I was white, female, and a bit older than my peers.

My caring and my ability to listen were crucial to my success. Also, my compassion for the artists and my sense of fairness. I believe that artists are unfairly oppressed in this industry, and I have made a change in the way business is done. I negotiated some of the best deals in Urban Music because of my belief system. I also believe my ability to teach and show others a better way was one of my strengths. I've always been able to translate complex ideas and concepts easily to make them simpler to understand. Combined with my honesty and transparency, people always have trusted me. And my track record reflects this.

I have always loved music. It's the soundtrack to my life. I remember riding around on my bike as a kid in elementary school with a radio tied to my handlebars. I had music everywhere I went, even though it was not a staple growing up in my home. My first album was given to me for free when I bought a pair of shoes (it was a promotion at the shoe store). I bought the shoes to get the free album. I was just a kid... maybe 13 or 14 or so. And oh, how those shoes hurt my feet.

The first Hip Hop song I fell in love with was Grandmaster Flash and the Furious Five...*Don't push me 'cause I'm close to the edge...* that sparked it all. It was live in concert at University of Pennsylvania. I was there to see The Psychedelic Furs and Grandmaster Flash was the opening act. Go figure! I met Richard Butler, the lead singer from the Psychedelic Furs, in a restaurant in New York in the 90s and told him of that moment when his concert changed my life. He told me he doubted it changed my life but thanked me for being kind. Not only did it change my life, but the lives of many, many Rap artists. If he only knew...

I have worked with hundreds of rappers over the past 25 years, and Rap Coalition has always answered to a Board Of Advisors which reads as a veritable Who's Who in the Rap music industry, consisting of Chuck D from Public Enemy, Vinnie from Naughty By Nature, David Banner, Keith Murray, Young Buck, Gipp from Goodie Mob, Too Short, Ras Kass, Do Or Die, Pimp C from UGK, Easy Mo Bee, C-Murder, B.G., KLC from Beats By The Pound, 8Ball, MJG, Shawty Redd, Evil Dee from Black Moon, Brotha Lynch Hung, Bizzy Bone, Mannie Fresh and Schoolly D. Prior to his death, Tupac Shakur was the first member of Rap Coalition's Board of Advisors. Rap Coalition is currently based in Atlanta, having relocated from New York City in 2005.

Through my company, PowerMoves, one of my personal priorities is to consult and help build regional and national independent Urban record labels so artists can regain control of their own art form. I've worked with Cash Money Records, Machine Gun Kelly (MGK), David Banner, Fiend, Young Buck, Young Jeezy's Corporate Thugz Entertainment (CTE), No Limit Records, C-Murder, Do Or Die, Trill Entertainment (Lil Boosie & Webbie), BloodRaw, DJ Screw, Trae Tha Truth, TMI Boyz Records, Think It's A Game (Rich Homie Quan, YFN Lucci, Trinidad James), Trouble's DuctTape, and many others.

In 2009, TMI Boyz had the distinction of being the #2 independent record label in any genre of music according to Nielsen and *Billboard* Magazine. I have helped build and mentored many of the successful indie labels that still exist in Rap today.

Consistent with this goal, I have negotiated stellar distribution deals in Urban music. I played a part in Eminem's deal at Aftermath/Interscope, Master P's No Limit deal with Priority Records, UGK's renegotiation with Jive Records, and Ruff Ryder's renegotiation with Interscope. I negotiated the incredible joint venture deal for Twista with Atlantic Records in 1996, which both *The Source* and *Rap Pages* magazines called "the best deal in the history of Black music." I then topped my own record with the now famous $30 million dollar deal for Cash Money Records with Universal. My focus is complete control and ownership for the independent labels or artists I represent. Master P was the first artist to keep control and ownership of 100% of his masters for No Limit.

The artists who became superstars had great music, incredible charisma, "IT" factor, a strong team around them, an incredible work ethic, and a budget supplied either by an investor or a record label. They needed all of this to succeed. Those who have "IT" are obvious. People attract to them like moths to light.

The most challenging part of my job was knowing that most artists lacked a part of what is necessary to succeed. It was always frustrating to know their dream could be deferred by lack of money, or the wrong team member on board, or mediocre music that fans didn't embrace. Another aggravation was the amount of inept and shady people that have always existed in the music industry. It seems like the music industry attracts an inordinate amount of people who either cannot do a job and say that they can, or who go out of their way to purposely fleece people out of their money. Perhaps it's the low barrier to entry that exists in the music industry, but any idiot with a budget to print business cards can say that they do a certain job, and very rarely will someone hiring them check them out to see if they're legitimate or not. Tens of millions of dollars are lost to scams and ineptitude in this industry. It really sucks!

I can't really name challenges that I have faced as a female in the music industry. I mean I'm not naïve, I am sure being female has impacted me negatively, it's just that I do not focus on it. My philosophy has always been to make a list of goals, put blinders on, and then focus on achieving those goals. And that has worked for me. It works wonderfully! So again, I realize that I have probably lost opportunities and I realize that perhaps people have not taken me as seriously as they would a man, or perhaps even an African American man, but it has never stopped me, it has never slowed me down, and it has never been an excuse for me. I just keep it moving. Fuck it!

I have never had a champion or a mentor in the industry. I have learned a lot from many, many, many people in the music industry, and I have had many people leak me inside information so that I could help artists succeed. But I have never had an actual champion or mentor. Having said that, I have mentored and championed MANY people in the music industry.

I am most certain that I have felt like quitting many times. But I can't recall any time where it was a serious thought, or serious contemplation. I never quit because I haven't finished what I started. I have a mission that I am accomplishing, a higher calling if you will. You don't quit that. Besides what else would I do? This is all I want to do.

I have burned out from time to time, but I have never quit. And I don't plan to.

There so many moments that have been gratifying that it's hard for me to narrow it down to one. But I guess if I had to share one moment, it would be my friendship with Tupac Shakur. He was an amazing human being and I had never met someone before him that I felt was so like-minded. He made an impact on me personally, and on Rap Coalition. He was someone that I knew I could really help, and I got the opportunity to do so.

One of the more challenging moments in my career happened after playing a role in the discovery of Eminem. I realized over time that the music industry is full of revisionist history. It's amazing to me, how depending upon who tells the story, how small and downplayed my role in his early career has become over time. I'm not quite sure why that is or why the head of a major record label has chosen not to tell the truth, even when confronted with the truth on film by researchers, but it is something that exists, and I have had to learn to live with. My role went from Entertainment Tonight calling me in the late 90s for a quote about Eminem at his direction (he told them he wouldn't do an interview about his early years unless they spoke with me), to books and HBO specials that barely mentioned my existence. I began to wonder in the mid-2000s who I must have pissed-off in his camp after being told by Paul Rosenberg in the 90s that he gave the first Platinum Plaque to me. (*Kanye shrug)

Every day that I do what I do is a great accomplishment because I really love what I do. I have gotten to impact some amazing people and to help build some amazing careers, and the opportunity to make a difference in the rap music business. I'm so fortunate to live the life that I live. There so many people that go into building a successful artist. There is no one moment. There is no one person. Understanding this is most likely my greatest accomplishment.

Helping people build successful careers is undoubtedly the best part of my job. I get to build millionaires. I get to help make a difference in people's lives and I see it every day. It is awesome and I continually rise to the challenge. I get to work with artists when they're brand new and nobody really knows who they are, and I get to help them build fame and wealth and popularity. Once they are stars, I no longer work with them because it's no longer fun. I really enjoy the grind and the build.

I have the type of personality that focuses on the ones that got away not the successes, I focus on what needs to get done not what has been achieved, and I focus on the losses not the wins. So, it's not in my nature to have noticed when things went well. But I guess the Cash Money deal was one of the instances where I realized that things went pretty well. It was hard to ignore all of the people coming at me to do the same type of deal for them which was impossible, and it was hard to ignore all of the interview requests that I was receiving.

It gives me the warm fuzzies when I see the artists and the labels that I have helped create, have stayed relevant. But every new success gives me a new high. The truth is I'm more surprised at the fact that I've been able to stay relevant in the music industry.

I'm still in love with the music that I helped create. I love it when I hear on the radio, and I love it when I hear it streaming in my house. And I especially love seeing a new generation of people and fans reacting to it. There are those warm fuzzies again.

I did not realize that there were Biopics being made that have left women out. I have noticed that I have been left out in many cases, but it never struck me as that having been done because I'm female. I always assumed that the revisionist history was so someone else could take full credit for the work that I, and others, had done. I don't believe it has anything to do with me being female, or white, or any of the other reasons that one could name. I think many people who have power in the music industry have giant size egos and those egos need to be stroked by receiving accolades. I've never been one to live on accolades. I am moved by successes and results, personally. And that's a good thing, because if you wait around for the accolades, you will be sorely disappointed in the music business.

I think the best advice that I can share with anyone, especially women, about navigating the music industry is to not fuck where you work. Once you are viewed as a sexual being, it makes it very difficult to get things done. Additionally, don't get bogged down by whether you're being treated fairly or unfairly as a woman but focus on getting the work done: Make a list of your goals and achieve them one by one. Everything else is a distraction. Lastly, learn as much as you can about the music industry. Most people don't take the time to do that and make a ton of mistakes. If you learn how the industry works you will be ahead of everyone else.

If I could give my younger self one piece of advice as I embarked upon my music journey, I would have told myself to build stronger and better relationships. I did too much on my own and did not depend upon others. This was costly for me. In hindsight, I should have depended upon my own network of people, and this would have made success far easier for me.

Each year since 1996, I have consulted at least two or more independent artists or indie labels, and through monthly panel discussions, my blog found on IndustryReport.com, my How To Get A Record Deal books, YouTube channel show "This Is Wendy Day", and my podcast called "The Cheat Code."

Happily, 25 years later, I'm still very active and relevant in the music industry. I am even more of an artist advocate (if that's possible), but now I help rappers and producers make money with their music independently while they retain ownership and control of their art form of music. In 1992, I started the not-for-profit organization as my way of giving back for all the happiness the music brought to me personally over the years. So, after all of these years in the industry, helping artists succeed is still my #1 agenda. I am honored to still be working and relevant in the Urban Music industry today, which is rare and amazing.

Wendy Day with David Banner

Mic Check 11

"I'll Have Your Job One Day"

~by~

Johnna Lister

The education to prepare me for the entertainment industry was local radio, good 70s and 80s TV, *Jet Magazine,* and the streets of Houston. I used to call the local radio stations to try to win stuff regularly. Once, I called in and sang the Popeye's jingle and won a ping pong set—we happened to have a raggedy pool table. (I guess there must have been a Christmas those were on sale. My parents weren't overpaying on that.)

When I went to the radio station to pick up my prize - KYOK AM I believe - I told the on-air DJ that I would have his job one day. He went on to be in position at corporate radio in larger markets and capacities years later. It was Steve Hegwood.

At 16, I was a photographer with my best friend Stephanie Gayle at Astroworld - the now gone Six Flags property in Houston. We would go to all of the concerts that came - LL, Heavy D, Joeski Love, Whodini, UTFO, FULL FORCE, Lisa Lisa & Cult Jam, Kool Moe

to: Johnna Lister with
eto Boys: Willie D &
Scarface

Dee, The Real Roxanne. We'd go to The Summit—former home of the Houston Rockets and current home of Joel Osteen and Lakewood church—and catch everything we could—Run DMC, Public Enemy, and the Beastie Boys. We were committed!! We spent whatever on tickets and did what we had to do.

We would read the back of album covers and call labels to find out when artists were touring, and ticket on-sale dates. There was no internet - you had to get the information from a PERSON if you didn't want to wait for them to advertise on radio. I was front row center over and over for Hip Hop shows. Run DMC, Public Enemy, Beastie Boys. I had floor seats for MC Hammer's big ass production.

We stood near stages and DJ booths at The Rhinestone Wrangler, The Rock, Main Event, and Thunderdome with Easy E, The Ghetto Boys, Wicket Cricket, Captain Jack ("Don't Do It Like That Baby!!") Chilly Bill Smith, and many others.

My first paying job was as a receptionist at a well-known hair salon in West Houston. Fondren area. Earvin & Co. In Houston, Black Hair is and has always been BIG BUSINESS. The entrepreneurial spirit is rampant. I was fortunate to be exposed to that type of grind and business acumen early. That also is what I think gave me the "get it out the dirt" hustle.

My next job was a hostess then waitress at JoJo's of Texas—a local diner style family restaurant in a Jewish neighborhood in South West Houston. This was the first time I experienced racism. A couple told my manager that they didn't want the "colored girl" waiting on them. This was also my first exposure to transgender folks—my friend Sylvia. A large, freckled, red-headed Black woman who fathered sons before she became Sylvia. She was one of my trainers and one of the kindest people ever. She passed away in the early 90's. Equally as poignant at that time in my life were my customers Mike, Naomi and Reuben.

Mike was a mentally challenged older man who liked to drink so we had to take care of him a bit. He loved us and he loved the restaurant. And we loved Mike.

Now Naomi and Reuben were a walking love story. A beautiful older Jewish couple who were rarely apart. Reuben was a Holocaust survivor. He taught 17-year-old me about the numbers on his arm, what he had been through, and how grateful he was to be alive and in Houston. I wouldn't fully understand the impact these people had on me until years later. In many ways, it really was THAT job which taught me so much about people and feelings, tolerance, co-existence, embracing and celebrating differences and how to choose to just be a kind human being—in spite of your circumstances or how people may treat you. I also learned how to cuss in Spanish—thanks to our kitchen crew.

I graduated from High school and went to Tuskegee University. I got involved with Student Government and would play records in the student center in between classes. One summer, I had an on-campus job with the SGA and the student body president at that time got me involved with his quest to bring a concert to the school. He said he knew someone from the community who would finance the whole thing and asked me to do the legwork ahead of a meeting with this person. I set out to speak to as many record labels, booking agents and managers as I could. I got rates, dates, and requirements. I also consolidated info on permitting, security, ground transportation, and anything associated with bringing a show to a college in the country. We had the ammunition we needed to make a great presentation to this anonymous citizen in the community.

The SGA president set up a meeting, told me to bring all of the info and that we would close this deal. During this "meeting", the SGA president proceeded to LITERALLY step on my toes under the table EVERY time I attempted to speak. He took all of my work, presented it as his own and treated me as if I was there to carry his bags. Well, as it turns out, his sponsor was a chain-smoking older woman whose boyfriend was a local drug dealer so nothing ever came of this meeting—except that I vowed I would never let a man - never let anyone - silence me, use me, or steal my work again.

After graduating from Tuskegee, I was home for two weeks and got a call from a friend of mine to come and help him with his new record label in New York. He had recently signed a white Reggae artist from Toronto—SNOW—and he needed someone to assist in running the management office and label. That was my first real music industry job.

Over time, growing pains of the business spilled into my friendship and it was time for me to move on.

I bartended, cashiered, and did all I could to remain afloat until I got a chance to temp at Sony Music. Someone in a different department overheard me covering phones and gave me an opportunity to interview with them. I landed a Video Assistant job. Five months later our label—The WORK Group—split from Columbia Records. Well, what I should say is that they kicked us off their floor. Then, my direct manager was fired. So, I was an assistant with no boss in a video department. I didn't have an office, a TV nor a VCR. But I proceeded to do the Video Manager job - without being asked, working for people whom I had never met as they were based in LA. I was getting videos played on MTV, BET and VH1 as well as several local outlets and I couldn't even watch any of it. I would get on the promotion calls and give the information with not much feedback. Finally, on one of the calls, one of the Presidents of the label asked, "Who are you??" I explained that I was an assistant that had been left behind and that I had been getting all of our videos played. They flew into town to meet me, gave me the job, an office, and a VCR.

I left The WORK Group and went into Video Programming at The Box Music Network as a Music Director. When The Box was bought by Viacom, I was brought on by MTV as a Director of Music and Talent. That position was arguably the most valuable—during that time, getting a job there was like sitting in a golden tower. For me, the value in it was access to the real decision makers in the business. I got job offers from Puffy, talent agencies and other labels. I eventually went over to Warner Brothers to do Marketing.

Six months into my two-year contract at Warner Bros., I was laid off. It was right after 9/11 and I was pregnant. That was pretty shocking, but it opened the door for me to do some things independently. I was given an opportunity by my original Video Promo boss—Gary Fisher—to work some videos for him. That gave me the flexibility to be home with my young children but also stay connected to the industry that I was so passionate about. I would go on to do Indie Video Promotion and Street Marketing for other labels and artists. That was a great time for me.

My last stop on the Music Biz ride was with Mathew Knowles. I had done some independent promotion for him during the time he was at Sanctuary Records. When he decided to walk away from that, he asked me to move back to Houston and help him run the management company and the Music World label. That two years was certainly full of wins and losses but lessons for sure. After being laid off from there—along with many people I brought on—I made the decision to move on. But hey—making Beyonce your last artist is the way to go out.

My greatest strength throughout my time in the industry was staying focused on the purpose—exposing good music. I didn't get caught up in the "how can I PERSONALLY cash in" mentality. There were times when people were cutting side deals, pushing, and prioritizing things that shouldn't see the light of day. I fought for the music that deserved it. I can recall music meetings where I would be the only person fighting for an artist or a song that nobody else seemed to get. I fought for Cher "Believe" when everyone said she was old and over. We were the first outlet to play the song and were on it for weeks before anyone else cared. It is still her biggest hit. One of my bosses told me that *The Miseducation of Lauryn Hill* was hype and made me bet my job when I pushed him on it. We all know how that worked out. Conversely, when something was trash—I was verbal about it. Generally, promo people don't think it's a good idea to say anything negative about a song on the promo call. Guess what? If I tell you it stinks, when it tanks I won't be held accountable for not getting the spins. So overall, riding with the good stuff and fighting for it was my calling.

I can't remember not being in love with music. I danced at weddings with my dad, I danced when company came over to entertain them. I listened to the radio nonstop and I played my dad's records on the record player. Nothing was better than that. Still nothing is better.

Music was my comfort zone. It was something I could get lost in. It was always connected to something good—even the songs that made me cry. It wasn't that I was sad—it was that I was touched by it. It would trigger memories. I could play songs over and over. I love the record store. I loved music magazines. I loved live concerts. I loved all genres.

The first rap song I fell in love with was OF COURSE "Rapper's Delight." It was as undeniable then as it is now. I learned every word!! My first favorite R&B song is actually instrumental—"Moments In Love" was a Quiet Storm staple. I used to sleep with my radio on all night—just loud enough for me to hear it, too soft for my mom to know it was on. I was probably 13 when Art of Noise released that song, but it became my instant fave. I was mesmerized by the transitions, the instruments moving in and out. For some people this is electronic music. For me, it was CLEARLY R&B—Black Radio Gold. Second to that was "Computer Love." Back when we used to slow dance. I don't have an all-time favorite jam—that is impossible for me.

Some of the artists I've had the pleasure of working with are Snow, Lyfe Jennings, Fiona Apple, The Fugees (collectively and individually), Beyonce, Destiny's Child, Solange, Diana King, Jamiroquai, John Legend, Bustah Rhymes, The Track Masterz, Puffy, Xzibit, Boney James, Puff Johnson, Leelah James—again—because of my positons at The Box and MTV—I really came in contact with several artists of all genres.

The "IT" factor starts with the music. There had to be something about the music that resonated for me to be on board. After that though, it was the passion and the grind. The artists who got the most traction were the ones who were willing to get into the trenches with us and get the groundwork done.

Jamiroquai and Fiona Apple were probably the artists that I was ready to go to war far. They were brilliant, they were unique, and they were both difficult projects to work. I was a Black girl working what—at the time—was considered an alternative artist in the marketplace. We worked Shadow Boxer for a FULL YEAR. We were relentless. Jamiroquai was an international artist that America had ignored for a full three album cycles. What a great challenge. This was literally the most challenging yet most fulfilling time of my life. Jamiroquai was the most played artist on BET at one point. Both artists went on to huge wins at the MTV awards that year—and that night Ol Dirty Bastard hit on me. I was winning! Ha!

The most frustrating thing about Fiona was that she was young and yet wise beyond her years. She was known to have temper tantrums and breakdowns—which she once did during a $16k live shoot of one of her concerts. I have an hour of footage of her pounding her piano and singing in tears while shooting the bird to five cameras at once. Yes—that happened!

The most frustrating thing about my career in the music industry was being slept on. People argued with me about the value of video. They dismissed me when I was at The BOX if they didn't have that outlet on their cable system. Some people didn't want to talk about Black music with the Black girl who also worked rock records. There were times when people were very dismissive. They assumed things. My how the tables and the tone turned when I got to MTV! People who told me I wasn't going to be valuable ended up on the other side of my desk begging for spins.

There were moments where male managers sought to bypass me in hopes that they could get more done with my male counterparts. As well, there were male execs who would have liked to relegate me to more administrative roles—until they saw me handle my business. I always stayed focused on the goal—get good music made and played. If that isn't what we are doing, why are we here?

I was the first Black person at The WORK Group. That was no challenge—the culture at that company was inclusive and respectful. I'd like to believe the only reason I was the first was because they simply hadn't met anyone who was willing to take on rock, alternative, AND Black music at once. Who knows. However, I was welcomed, appreciated, and supported. And my response to that was that I broke artists. I stayed focused on the music and the artists and the goals in front of us. I always thought to myself, *When I break this artist, you WILL respect me.*

There was once a female who attempted to undermine my talent. I had a coworker who assumed I would become her surrogate when the label created an official video "department". She told me I would need to decide if I wanted to report to her or to the radio promo VP. I proceeded to create a 7-page document which detailed how the new department would run and the processes involved for getting video play and subsequently selling records—and I submitted it to the GM and the Presidents. I reported directly to the top. Next?

Jeff Ayeroff and Demette Guidry are the two people who gave me my best opportunities in the business. I am happy to have a list of people I could go to for sound advice—my two best friend Stephanie Gayle and Mona Scott-Young were of course my everyday go to people. We were all scratching it out back then, so we leaned on each other.

I never felt that I wanted to quit. It just wasn't an option. I had goals to be successful in the music industry. The moment that makes me smile even until today is that I was able to see Biggie and Tupac perform "Party and Bullshit" live at The Palladium. That night was epic.

I would say that my greatest accomplishment was dismantling an attempt by Madonna to force MTV's hand in playing a violent video of hers. We had a first right of refusal agreement with top tier artists. She refused to make edits to a very graphic, violent video—banking on the thought that we would pass on it—and her plan was to let HBO premier it ahead of the Soprano's season opening. I figured out her scheme and we played it once—with a disclaimer.

My most embarrassing moment was when I was about seven, I fell in Sears, my panties were showing under my dress and two older white men behind me laughed. This stuck with me for years—grownups would laugh at a child—instead of helping her up. So—that taught me—nobody is going to pick you up when you fall—they may even laugh at you. Shit happens. Just wear clean panties.

The aspect of the job that I enjoyed the most was setting goals with the artist and accomplishing them and being able to celebrate that later. It was always cool to make the call and say—we got the add or we hit the Top 10. I am always proud and excited to see my artists. It's always like running into family. Hearing the songs on the radio always brings feelings of pride. There is a type of ownership.

I was clear I was certified a Rockstar behind the Mic when the Music Department at MTV gave me my going away party and the top three executives of the entire company showed up to send me off. The department was shocked—I was told confidentially that it had NEVER happened before. As a matter of fact, the president told me she "fucked up" by letting me get away.

My hope for the people who tell stories is that they recognizing that the whole story has to be presented. It's disappointing that in this day and time that the women are still being edited out. It makes no sense.

The one thing I would advise a young woman entering the industry would be—know who you are before you arrive—and don't compromise that. Having values and principles often create a longer path to success but there is nothing wrong with that. If you do not compromise yourself, you can arrive at your destination whole and with your soul intact. That is PRICELESS.

If I had an opportunity to guide my younger self, I would tell her "You may not believe this, but one day this amusement park called the music industry will be your past. You won't even miss it. Your biggest challenge will be what to do next. It will take some time but that's okay. Just trust that when you left the industry behind you didn't leave your spark. Be patient and someone is going to see that you are still an amazing human. Don't throw in the towel and doubt yourself. Your life will always have purpose and fulfillment."

After my stint with Mathew, I was just tired of "the game". I could not even listen to the radio. I spent the next two years listening only to sports talk. Partially due to the culture at the company, partially due to the game changing so drastically and I found myself facing things that I deemed unhealthy to a family life and to my inner peace. It was an easy decision to not return after giving so much for so long. After some time, I was able to settle back into being a fan, buying music and listening to it and soaking it in again. There was no pressure to win—only to love the music again—the way I used to when I was the kid calling the radio station.

new yo
UN DMC

Mic Check 12

"Keep It Moving"

~by~

Kymberlee Thornton

Hello, I am Kimberly Thornton -aka- Kymberlee "Pump It Hottie" Thornton and I have had a love for music since I was a child. I had the interest and ambition of the entertainment business as a fan, enthusiast, musician, and a dancer with an overall goal to become a Record Label & Entertainment Executive. specifically in the areas of A&R, Artist Development, Music Publishing and Recording Engineering. Studying music at the gifted School For The Creative & Performing Arts, since grade school prepared me to research the various departments of the record labels and recording studios in California & New York as a teenager from home.

My career path was set at a very young age as I entered The School For Creative & Performing Arts where I was able to interact with young people of all ages since the school ranged from grades 4-12. The school helped to mature me and prepared me for a career-oriented lifestyle

)to: Kymberlee Thorton
h Darryl McDaniels of
Run-DMC

in the arts. We learned the vastness of the world through our classes, performances, and character-building exercises. We also learned quite early that following the right virtues would increase our possibilities for success. This was instilled early in our school years and the vocational classes taken through a top satellite academic school prepared me with the office skills necessary for my corporate trajectory.

I had a huge social life in Cincinnati, and it was an asset to have a natural dance skill that afforded me to be as they say in the mix of my city for various clubs, concerts and local groups. I was lucky to have the history and sound of Cincinnati right in my own home. I grew up with my aunt Shirley Grant who was the first secretary of Cadillac Records and was also the assistant to James Brown. My mother was a fashion model and had the friendships of Al Jarreau, Minnie Riperton, Nikki Giovanni, and Randy Crawford. It was also great as a child always spending some summers with my older cousins in Dayton Ohio where I lived prior to Cincinnati. Those cousins gave me the most history, as I did not know that my mother's cousin was Leroy "SugarFoot" Bonner of the Ohio Players. I just knew there was always music, a recording studio in the house, lots of socialization, kids, and instruments around. The times I have had around all those influences help me to shape my education and career in the direction of a Record Label Executive. I even started reading liner notes as a child musician.

As a child I fell in love with music, as I understood how lyrics and music connected people of different backgrounds. I knew music made everyone happy and was a constant at gatherings with family and friends. My whole family was devoted to constant music playing throughout the house. There were but only a few networks in my time and my family chose to rarely watch TV, but to always have music playing in the house.

Growing up music was a hobby, investment and overall took up the majority of my studies in school. At SCPA there were several classes related to playing instruments. Homework was rehearsing for band, orchestra, and performances. Most of my associates in high school and after high school were working musicians, involved in Hip Hop from DJ's, break-dancers and choreographers. That was pretty much my social circle since school.

I played piano as a child and by age 11, I started playing clarinet and soon switched from public school to The School For the Creative & Performing Arts of Cincinnati was the very first pilot for the Performing Arts Schools nationally. I majored in Music & held Drama as my minor. At SCPA I was able to study classes in music theory, woodwinds, and orchestra as well as classes related to all areas of acting, staging, costume, make-up and set design. A few years later I switched over to a satellite college prep academic school in the interest of taking up a vocational program geared towards Business/Stenography/Office Secretarial skills. I simultaneously maintained a position as first clarinet in the school marching band and orchestra and also as a competitive varsity cheerleader, later attending UCLA for Recording Engineering in 1987.

The first Hip Hop song I remember is "Rapper's Delight". I found it to be catchy and I enjoyed the sample, which was by one of my favorite groups Chic. But, I was not a fan of that particular song, I think my favorite at that time that really stuck to me was "Christmas Rapping" by Kurtis Blow then "The Message" by GrandMaster Flash & the Furious Five. Those were my favorites when rap first came out. My all-time favorite R&B jam must be shared between 2 separate spectrums "Knee Deep" & Marvin Gaye's "I Want You"). My first R&B songs would be early Stevie Wonder "Finger Tips" & The Supremes' "Symphony", and The Jackson's 5 "Rocking Robin".

I have worked in the recording industry well over 30 years and the TV/Film & Live Event industries for over 10 years. Working in choreography, marketing, promotions, product placement, product management, casting, recording, editing, tour management, special events, Artist & Repertoire, Music Publishing, Music Management, Branding and Staffing from a corporate level. I now serve as a business owner and freelancer in the recording and televised entertainment industries. I also design refurbished fur.

My History of Employment:

1984:

My introduction to the executive side of the record industry was as a secretary to The Pros Record Pool in Oakland, California. The Pros managed the Top 75 *Billboard* Chart Reporting DJ's on the West Coast of the country. In addition to that I doubled working at the legendary Escovedo's Nite Club as the Assistant Sound Engineer in the evening. I left the Pro's in 1986 to pursue schooling at UCLA, for classes in Designation of Recording Engineering. I became a mother in 1987 and took some time to spend with my son and family back in Cincinnati.

1988:

I was lucky to get an internship at Motown Records after constant persistence on my part with follow-ups to find a job through my strong contact base and support system I had in Oakland. Working with the talents of R&B artist Brenda Vaughn-who was working with Pebbles, Toni Tony Tone, Rosie Gaines, Denzil Foster & Thomas McElroy, Robert Brookins, En Vogue, Jay King, and Club owner Jeffrey Pete, was a big contribution to my own relationships with these talents as I developed the same supportive relationships with all. My status with The Pro's Record Pool & Escovedo's enhanced my relationships with those in the music industry in the Bay Area. It proved to be of great reliance and gave me greater support from my peers. Upon my quick return to Oakland, I immediately started as an intern in the North West Regional District under the Promotions & Marketing Department at Motown. I was soon promoted after a short 3 months to assistant for Chelle Seabron, West Coast Director of Promotions & Marketing of Motown Records. Over the next year I was promoted from the assistant of the Director to a status of North West Regional Manager of Marketing for Motown Records.

1989:

My former Motown boss Chelle fortunately convinced me, to interview with this new boutique company, quickly having great success with a single called, "Turn This Mother Out". The artist was a performer like no other rap artist. I decided not to return to school and take the opportunity to interview. I had broken sales records at Motown with artist Diana Ross, the *Do The Right Thing* Soundtrack, The Boys, and the R&B group Today, produced by Teddy Riley. So, I had become known with great relationships from my in-store marketing campaigns and DJ support through the major market radio directors.

The interview was a bit rough, but I took the job upon the immediate offering. I was employed as the National Director of Marketing for Bust-It Management. Bust-It had been successful with a leather brand named Troop and with the artist named M.C. Hammer, 2 Big MC and his dancers Oaktown 357. The CEO Louis Burrell had proposed to release a roster full of artists, which would include a new upcoming project for MC Hammer to be entitled *Please Hammer Don't Hurt Em.* It would be completed a solo project for the dancers Oaktown 357, R&B group Special Generation, Detroit rap group DBG's and others.

Switching from National Director of Marketing for Bust-It/Capitol to the department of Artist & Repertoire for the newly developed label was a natural progression and professional goal for me in our joint venture with Capitol Records where I took over the department of A&R services within the next years under Bust-It/Capitol Records, signing Doug E. Fresh to our imprint deal.

I collaborated in the structure of the label deal for Bust- It/Capitol Records - the first multi-million joint venture with a rap artist. Since I and only a few others had actual corporate record label experience, I was an asset to the newly formed company. My marketing ideas and insight on *Billboard* Reporting proved to be quite valuable to the company and the history of music as for myself. As Soundscan was then created over the time our artists maintained hold of the *Billboard* Charts. I was able to hire most of my own staff, work collectively with Capitol Records to ensure success of MC Hammer, and to grow his label's roster. Achieving The *Billboard* Record for Top album for 31 weeks at No. 1 with the *Please Hammer Don't Hurt Em*. Grossing over 33 million sales and multiple gold & platinum singles with that one project.

1993:

I had a near fatal car accident in my hometown of Cincinnati attending my maternal Aunt's funeral. Two young men were speed racing and crashed into my car. After a helicopter transport, flat lining, a coma, being wheelchair bound for seven months, and after almost a year of surgeries and rehabilitation, I decided to return to New York to once again reclaim to my career as a music industry executive.

1994:

Shortly after regaining the ability to walk again but not yet out of physical therapy or doctor care, I started interviewing in the music industry at the labels and publishing companies again with the support of my peers. I was hired as Manager of Creative Services for Jive Records Publishing entity Zomba Music Publishing.

1998:

I left Zomba Music Publishing. I began my company The Repertoire, a boutique company that represented various *Billboard* charting musicians, songwriters and producers as their primary agent or co-agent to various music production houses and assisting in artist placements, production, and publishing deals. Those talents included Rodney Jerkins, Malik Pendleton, Dahoud Darien, Frankie Romano, Dwayne Bastiany, James Glasco, The Character's, Tony Prendatt, and a host of others.

My greatest areas of strength have been in directing and developing the idea, being attentive to the detail and having an open mind. If I have just enough to work with, I can visually conceive a full concept visually. Creative Services, encompasses so much of my background in so many areas which has abled me to constantly create relationships with some of the most talented performers and some of the most intelligent colleagues in professional business. I know I have a great intuition regarding talent from my formal training and executive experience.

Some of the artists I have been blessed to work with are:

Midnight Star, Bernard Wright, Charlie Singleton, Bernie Worrell, Jeff Redd, Ivana Santilli, Levert, Donnie Osmond, Robert Brookins, Earth Wind & Fire, Kool Moe Dee, Tribe Called Quest, Shaquille O'Neal, Christina Aguilera, Kymani Marley, Faith Evans, Charlie Singleton, Bernard Wright, Espose, Cameo, Today, Diana Ross, Klymax, Loose Ends, Paris the Artist, Pete Escovedo, Whodini, Teddy Riley & Guy, Too Short, MC Hammer, Doug E. Fresh, Eric B. Full Force, Trey Songs, Carl Thomas, R. Kelly. I represented several musicians, songwriters and producers that afforded me to work with a numerous amount of talents and their catalogs. The list goes on as to the musicians, songwriters and producers that I have worked with and represented behind some of the top R&B, Dance, Pop & Hip Hop *Billboard* artists.

I can always tell an artist will be a star when there is more than just that one thing about them that piques my interest. A look, a sound anything that is different from what is in the market currently. Someone that stands out for all the good reasons. Talents that were multi-faceted and multi-dimensional in the thinking of their artistry and catalog. The talents that listened, took the advice and were openly willing to collaborate and stay disciplined for their craft and goal were those that we still see today.

Upon, moving to New York to open the East Coast offices of Bust-It/Capitol Records, it was important for me to sign a known artist with a strong Hip Hop catalog. I felt that it was many complaints of those in the Hip Hop industry that felt as though MC Hammer was not a valid rap artist. The music industry seemed to be going in a new direction in musical sound and Hip Hop from the East Coast was lasting. I had the opportunity to meet with Doug E. Fresh, who at the time was not happy with his Danya/Fantasy contract. I made it a mission to bring a lyricist and performer of his caliber, credibility, and authenticity to our label.

Doug E. Fresh is known till this day all over the world as one of the Greatest Entertainers in Hip Hop! He has been a successful businessman in several businesses from restaurants, TV shows, executive producing, consulting producer as well many other business ventures. Doug is probably one of the most solid confirmations of my belief in a talent.

Upon signing Doug, I learned quickly how much he was influenced by the MC Hammer image and success. Doug created his first release with all the embellishments of a Hammer tour! His video and first single release, which I advised against both, was a Rick James sample as Hammer's. Doug even had on a gold leather Hammer suit with embellishments. I turned in a resignation letter I was so frustrated.

My letter was not honored. But, I was able to redeem his project, my good name, and career by changing the whole creative direction of his project and image.

One of the most frustrating things I've encountered from a corporate standpoint is not having full signature authority, only co-authority to sign. Sexism and racism also are pervasive, which has been a stumbling block for all women. I have rarely seen women in Presidential roles at labels, Lisa Cortes, Glynice Coleman, Sylvia Rhone, Sharon Heyward, and Cassandra Mills are of the only names of women of color that were holding those titles back then. Absurd in an industry so large only a handful of women in such powerful positions just do not equate.

I was fortunate to have several champions and mentors that I would have to grant credit. Many were women as it is today, Brenda Vaughn, Juanita Escovedo, Chelle Seabron, Vivian Scott-Chew, Lisa Cortes, Audra Washington, Nicole Scott, and Glynice Coleman just to name a few that continually encouraged me, pushed me, and many times cheered me toward a direction they saw was a good fit for me.

The one time I felt like an absolute ROCKSTAR behind the mic was when I arrived at Escovedo's as a young eager intern as assistant to the sound guy hoping to just learn about sound staging. One day he was delayed, and I had to start the sound for Tito Puente! I thought to myself, *How exciting this is as a teenager to direct the sound board for such a legendary artist as Tito Puente and his orchestra at Sheila & Pete Escovedo's Night Club Escovedo's.* In that moment, I felt like I had arrived at my dream. I've always been around artist and saw them as regular folks, but Tito was an artist in a market I had not even considered. The amount of instruments he used on stage gave me no fear but sheer adrenaline to Mic up. The show was fantastic, and Tito spoke to me as Juanita Escovedo translated. I was working in Escovedo's, in charge of sound for Tito Puente, and Sheila E's mother who helped me get the job, was translating for Tito Puente and I. *Wow.*

The one moment that makes me cry even today is when I had my car accident in 1993, is how the music industry showed me a great deal of support. There were announcements placed in trades, there were trust funds set up for my medical and financial support. This was arranged by my friends at the labels and my childhood friends. The mere fact that I had such a unity of support during such a traumatic time was a blessing and I am always overwhelmed by the support given from those in the music industry. I am blessed as I reflect on the career choice I took and the relationships I made with so many colleagues all across the world. Thirty-plus years later I stay in contact with many from the music industry as I do with my childhood friends.

Sometimes, the nostalgia and emotion I get when I am in a club and hear a song I've been a part of simply gives me a feel-good sentiment all over. To see the crowd respond to any song I've worked on in a positive light just revives me and rejuvenates my Spirit. Although, the crowd does not know I was a part of the song that makes them sing I always feel like I am a part of each person's celebration knowing I played a part of that happiness.

When I see Biopics that don't actually give an accuracy of events, or I see many I know who served in positions that created the talents not being featured actually baffles me. It seems to be a disappointment to hear the stories narrated by others that may not have been as involved or fully involved. It always appears to be missing information that I want to scream at my TV to validate my colleagues.

When seeking out this business as a career choice, I would advise anyone to do his or her research. Investigate your field of interest; study the steps of those in positions. Join various membership groups, surround yourself in the environment in which you wish to grow. Continuously study your craft, keep your skill updated, and remember everything changes nothing stays the same so prepare always to keep it moving!

Keep It Moving is also the advice I would give my younger self. Focus on my own company versus the loyalty of someone else's company. If I had known as much about contract deals prior to Hammer's company versus learning in the position, I would have set up my own company immediately after breaking the *Billboard* record. After I knew many of the artist on our roster would not prove sales success, I should have resigned, but my loyalty and fear to leave left me struggling with the company just to get paid at the end.

Today, I'm currently working in TV/Film Production Management. Working in several areas of production from a production assistant, to a credentials coordinator, a production coordinator, dressing room coordinator, hair & make up tech. Working many top shows across the country from VH1's Story Teller's, VH1's UnPlugged, Rock & Roll Hall of Fame, Kid's Choice Awards, NBC's New Year's Countdown as well AMC's Comic Book Men with Kevin Smith. I have my own business, Keep It Moving Entertainment Group, a media content company representing all aspects of the entertainment from music to TV/film and fashion design in addition to representing all talent and tech behind the scenes.

THE most important survival skills I have found that I could not do without in this business is drive and determination, with them, you shall always be able to stand on your feet.

HOLLYWOOD
PRODUCTION
DIRECTOR
DATE

Mic Check 13

"You Are Enough"

~by~

Winsome Sinclair

I grew up in a Caribbean home (being from Jamaica) where my parents were always singing. playing music and even taught us how to dance. My parents played all types of music in our home from Sam Cooke, Otis Redding and Brooke Benton, to Nancy Wilson, Etta James, Mahalia Jackson to the Supremes, The Jackson 5, Barry White and McFadden & Whitehead. We loved it all even classical and country music. I fell in love with music as a child. My father was in a band in Jamaica before I was born. The love of music was in my DNA. I played the piano as a child and studied at both Brooklyn College and Carnegie Hall. Music always had the power to shift my mood and touch my soul. Music helped me to express things I wasn't verbally confident to communicate. I still associate songs and soundtracks with time periods in my life and what I was going through at the time. The first Rap song I loved "**Rapper's Delight.**" I've had many favorites since then but my stand out favorite would still have to be **"I Ain't No Joke" by Eric B & Rakim.**

After graduating from FIT in spring 1985 I attended FAMU (Florida Agricultural & Mechanical University) one of the nation's great HBCUs from spring 1986/to spring 1989. When I left FAMU, I didn't know what I wanted to do as a career but ever since I was a child, I knew my life's work would be something I loved so much I would do it for free, and it would be something that made other people's dreams come true. Once I left FAMU and moved back to Long Island, I began my search for a traditional entry level job in banking or insurance. After having no luck a girlfriend of mine (Dee) gave me **Spike Lee's** mailing address. I wrote Spike a letter the week Do the Right Thing premiered. In the letter I asked him for the opportunity to learn. Two days later his executive producer Jon Kilik called and offered me an internship on Spikes next film. In fall 1989 I interned in the extras casting department on the film **Mo Better Blues. I** then continued to work on all Spikes films for the next 23 years.

Today my company Winsome Sinclair and Associates still does casting for the film, TV, and music video industry. My greatest area of strength was loving my work and feeling compelled to bring my "A" game every time. Film was my start but I definitely wasn't prepared for the Music industry. The fact that I love music and always will, is the aspect of the job that I most enjoyed. The only commonality between film and music for me is loving your work and the work ethic my parents instilled in me to do your BEST at all times

Some of the music artists I've worked with are **Tupac Shakur, Busta Rhymes, Salt-N-Pepa, Nas, Run DMC ,LL Cool J, Mariah Carey, Diddy, Mob Deep, Little Kim, Black Rob, DMX, Method Man, Whitney Houston, Man, Mary J. Blige, Alicia Keys, Snoop Dogg, Ice Cube, Beyoncé, Jay Z** and too many others to list here. I loved seeing all of their video's premiere on BET and MTV. It was a joy to work with them. I could tell who was on the superstar trajectory. For me they just glowed. I remember this about Tupac, Busta Rhymes, and DMX because I was in the casting department for all their first films. I also remember seeing this on Alicia Keys as my company cast the first music videos from her debut album.

Tupac was one of my most memorable artist to work with . As a young man I remember he was compassionate, uber talented and full of energy. He was born to be brilliant and make a difference. Even in his youth you saw the fire of wisdom beyond his years. I will always remember after we completed filming the movie **Juice**, I reached out to PAC and asked him to speak to a group of troubled youth my brother was mentoring. He did not even hesitate to say, "Yes." His heart was BIG and he had a burden for his people and especially the youth. Having had the experience of working with PAC on his first film . I was honored many years later when I was called upon to cast the movie about his life **All Eyez On Me.**

While there were many ups and downs (thankfully more ups than downs) in my career the most frustrating part of this career was managing the large personalities and the pitfalls of the groupies who were willing to do anything to get noticed for their 15 minutes of fame. It's during these times that prayer and wisdom had to prevail. I remember wanting to quit while in the middle of making a major film. I handed in my resignation while working on the film **Malcolm X** after I was physically assaulted by a male actor. That was the last straw for me. No job was worth my safety. That night I had a serious talk with GOD. Instead of resigning I ended up staying on to complete the film for one reason alone. I stayed because I did not want to look in the mirror for the rest of my life and see a quitter looking back at me. I'm glad I stayed. I had a destiny to fulfill . Now when I see artists that are still relevant today, knowing I helped to set their course I feel blessed to do what I love for a living. When I hear the songs on the radio and see the music videos that I worked on, I still turn it up the volume and dance. It's a good feeling to know that you were a part of making history.

As a woman, one of the biggest challenges I faced in the industry was maintaining respect as a businesswoman given the environment we had to work in . Through the language of some hip hop songs and videos , women would often be devalued, diminished, and sometimes disrespected. How do you maintain your dignity as a BOSS in that environment? I was able to overcome those challenges through a lot of Prayer!!! Staying grounded with friends, and remembering your job is what you do, not who you are. My personal goal is and was always to leave a situation better than how I found it. I never considered being a woman a negative. In fact I consider it to be my super power. I have always lead with my heart and given my best.

I have had a few champions in the industry whom I could count on for sound advice. These are the folks that believe in you, empower you and sometimes see more for you than you even see for yourself. When challenges were in my face I could always count on a handful of folks: my first partner/big sister Elloise Dover (RIP), my partner second partner Renton Kirk (RIP), Casting Director Jaki Brown and director John Singleton were my mentors. Eloise continuously reinforced all I could be and helped me to identify and honor the calling on my life. Renton gave me the courage to start my casting company in 1996 he helped me to dream a bigger dream for myself. I was more than a serial freelancer I was a business. Another contributor to my path was the producer and visionary Jon Marc Sandifer. He guided me to see that WSA was more than just my business it was my brand., I have also been blessed to have three dynamic mentors along the way, casting director Jaki Brown took me under her wing on **Juice** , director John Singleton (RIP) began mentoring me on the film **Higher Learning. Jaki and John** made spaces and created opportunities for me to grow and shine. It was Jaki Brown that recommended me to work with Hype Williams on the iconic hip hop film **Belly**. My third mentor was a powerful woman named Bunnie Jackson-Ransom. Bunnie began mentoring me when I co-produced the documentary MAYNARD. This documentary was based on her first husband's life and career. It was Bunnie that gave me the strategy to write and publish my first book.

I know my part in the history of Pop Culture. I also see how women have been left out in telling the history. I am however optimistic that our day will come...And it begins with projects like this one. We as women need to claim our space and tell our stories. We as women have done trailblazing work to get us to today. We follow in footsteps of our predecessors as we pave the way for the next generation. I understand the assignment and take it very seriously. We have come a long way but we still have a way to go. As we go, we must remember to leave a path for the women coming behind us through mentoring. Over the last 30+ years mentoring the next generation has always be a passion and a mandate I set for myself. I endeavor to be the mentor that I needed when I started out. I give the advice I needed to hear.

To my younger self, the one piece of advice I would tell myself is **You Are Enough.**

The advice I have for women wanting to enter the industry today is to keep your eyes on the future, while working hard and smart in the present. And, always remember don't do anything you can't tell your grandkids about!

I am blessed that after 30-plus years I'm still here. This is still my life, still casting and now producing. This is my ministry. This is where I serve.

My deepest regret? Not knowing/understanding my mission sooner.

Today, I am now a mother of two young kings (being raised on 90s Hip Hop LOL). I am a cancer survivor and running my own

Entertainment company WSA. We develop, cast, and produce films, and documentaries. We also nurture and consult with aspiring filmmakers. I am an author of the children's book YOU ARE MY SONshines, which is a love story for my sons on how we came to be a family through GOD and adoption. We are currently developing this book into a documentary and eventually an animated series. I belong to several organizations (CSA, AMPAS, NYWIFT. I also sit on several advisory boards (AAWIC, MMCA) and I serve as an adoption advocate through the NAA. In 2020 just prior to the pandemic shut down of the world I along with a former mentee launched our mentorship organization ICU Sis👀 💕 dedicated to pairing powerful mentors with extraordinary mentees.

Winsome Sinclair and Tupac Skakur

Mic Check 14

"Do What Inspires You"

~by~

Linda Haynes

I was the girl who wanted to be an actress, yet I was always in love with music. I had six siblings. My mother was a native New Yorker, actually my father was a native New Yorker too but his heritage was West Indian. Coming from the Jazz Age, when my father was home on Sunday, the music belonged to him. We couldn't put on our record player and we couldn't touch the radio. We had to listen to whatever it was he wanted to hear. He would put on Billie Holiday, Mozart, or Reggae. So, we all had an incredible appreciation for music.

During the week, when we had to do dishes the radio was on listening to Jocko. We liked to dance, we liked to listen to music. So, music was in my home, always. Always!

Yes, I was initially at Morgan State University in Maryland to study acting and I came back home because I accused my mother of not telling me that I was going South, and I *could not* stay there! I came back to New York; I went to the New Lafayette Theater School. I studied theater and drama classes. Then I went to the

New York School of Announcing and Speech because I figured I needed to get a job. I knew I had that I had kind of voice for commercials and some on-air work. A girlfriend said that Bob Law was looking for an assistant at WWRL Radio. and I went there for an interview, and he hired me that day. I thought I was going to be on the air at some point, but I wound up being his assistant, then producing the overnight talk show *Night Talk*, and then finally becoming the music director after Jerri Shannon.

I thought it was interesting that I was drawn to the radio station. and being on an AM radio station, "Wheew, what the hell? But I loved it. And people like the greats like Bobby Jay, Jerry Bledsoe, and Hank Spann... I mean, it was incredible. It was absolutely wonderful.

WWRL-AM 1600 was one of the premier R&B stations in the 70s and 80s. they existed before WBLS. The Chief Rocker Frankie Crocker came from WWRL, Jerry Bledsoe, and Vaughn Harper. It was considered a Power AM station. They were there first and when Inner-City Broadcasting established WBLS it was one of the first R&B stations FM stations in the New York City Tri-State area. All of the guys migrated to WBLS. I stayed at WWRL until Richard Smith at Arista Records offered me a job. He thought I would be a great fit since I was the music director seeing all of the label promotions people on my record days. I agreed. I went to work at Arista, but being a promotion person did not work for me.

I wound up coming back to my comfort zone of radio I was producing *Night Talk* again, and then I did an event about radio and the radio pioneers for Bob Law. It was at the Schomburg Library in Harlem. A lot of record label people came to the event including Sharon Heyward. She liked what I had done and offered me a job!

I know, what made me gravitate towards the record industry was more money. I had a little girl in private school that I had to pay for, and later in college. There was not enough money at the AM radio station. It was gratifying, and it certainly was a lot more money than my peers were making being in radio. But the financial leap to records was huge for me.

Sharon was at the brand-new VP at Virgin Records and was starting Virgin America. I said, "I don't know if I want to do that…" She said, "Please come in, see the people." Audrey Strahl was the head of promotions for Virgin America at that time. I came to the New York office and Sharon was in LA, we had a three-hour interview, and offered me the job. I actually started the R&B Publicity department for Virgin Records because my strong suit was definitely writing and communications.

When they opened their Virgin America Offices, there were a bunch of White people. With Sharon and the R&B department we had Ziggy Marley, Lenny Kravitz, and the brand-new group After 7 that were BabyFace's little brothers, then came Lalah Hathaway, Soul II Soul, and E.U. (Experience Unlimited).

The first time that we went to the UK we had Soul II Soul, and… were doing some events there and meeting the people in the UK office so they could see what we were doing while working with Boy George. When we got there Richard Branson was at the record shop! He was fabulous. He made people who worked for him feel like they were valued. I was really, really, really impressed with the organization that he ran. Now I understand how he evolved, and how he became the person that he was and is.

Other people began to notice my work because Michael Mitchell from Motown offered me a job as Vice President of Publicity. How does one refuse an offer from Motown!? Some of the artists I worked with during my Motown career were all of Biv Ten's artists, like Boyz II Men, Queen Latifah, and Johnny Gill.

Ms. Ross, she was extremely intimidating. Once, we were in a conference room the first time that I met her with all the senior executives of the label, including Jheryl Busby, Paris Ealy, and the heads of every department were sitting around the table. All for Ms. Ross. She was definitely drawn to the men. As we were leaving she says, "So Linda, how do you feel about that?" I didn't even know she noticed me or knew my name. That's what impressed me about her, she got it! She got all the dynamics in the room, and knew who you were, and what you were doing... and I was super-impressed. Because she didn't *have* to know. Miss Ross had the IT Factor oozing from her pores.

With my other artists, it was kind of difficult to determine their IT Factor right away. The first time that I saw Johnny Gill, I said, "Boy, what is wrong with you? Why do you look so LA ghetto?" But when he got on the stage, he was mesmerizing! That song "...Put On Your Red Dress" was just like an anthem! He was incredible.

Same thing with Boyz II Men, they were little boys, but when they got on the stage, they took your breath away. They were also incredible!

With Lalah Hathaway, she was so shy. She was almost like one of those people who would hold her head down and sing, but that voice! I said, "Girl, put your head up and let these people know who you are!" And she went on and became more of a star. But wow, when she started, she was like really the little girl in the room. Then she came more into her own. I don't know if everybody had that "It" thing, or if they developed it along the way. I think that if you have a degree of talent, then you can develop the stardom. You have to be willing to put in the work. Now, Queen Latifah demanded a room. When she walked in, everything about her screamed, "Uh-huh, I'm here. I'm here."

I would say After 7 was my favorite. First of all, because they were so cute. Second of all, because they wouldn't stay out of my office. They had a billion questions, and they wanted to know the business. Even though they came from LA, Reid and Babyface, they had a curiosity about the business. Then when I saw them traveling and performing, those little girls were throwing themselves in front of these boys, and they never lost their minds. They *never* lost their minds. I was extremely proud of them. I know that attributed to their success because if you get blinded by the light, you can lose your way. I think you have to develop a certain amount of arrogance, first of all you've got to have it to get on that stage, and they had it. They *had* it.

One of the most amazing events I got to coordinate was in Jamaica for *Motown Soul By The Sea.* We bought out an entire luxury resort. It was Jheryl Busby, Stevie Wonder, Temptations, and all the new artists that he was signing. Everybody who was on the label roster was there. We brought in all of the music publications, syndicated radio shows, and journalists. It was all filmed and was pretty wonderful.

The most frustrating part about my job when I moved to Motown, was they relocated me from New York to LA. And I had a home, my mom was with me, my daughter was with me. It killed me because my life was in New York for real. Busby said, "This is what we're doing, we're going to be on the West Coast." And so, I relocated to the West Coast. My mom went down South with my sister and my daughter got her own apartment. but she was miserable and wound up coming to LA with me.

Being in that West Coast environment was not for me. They wound up terminating me, but I wasn't unhappy. I was angry. Because they made me drop everything. I came into the office telling them, "Are you fucking kidding me? Y'all have to be out of your minds! I would've been very happy staying in New York and I could've gone someplace else. So, what is this?"

I don't think the world knows, they terminated me, but paid me for a year.

Being a woman was a challenge in radio and records. I would never say "me too" because I wasn't intimidated, thank God because I had brothers. So, I went through life feeling like I had a shield. But they would hit on you, and they would proposition you. You'd walk in a room and forget it if you were attractive, then you needed to talk with a shield and a gun. But the other part of it was I always had older guys, like Buddy Scott and Melvin Moore. They were like guardian angels for me. I had an incident with someone from an indie label. They came into my office and threatened me because I wasn't playing a certain record. They walked out of the office, and I was really shaken. They were talking about breaking legs and stuff, and I know it was done before. Those were the days when… things happened. You know, the wild, wild west. It just so happened that Buddy Scott called me and said, "What's the matter?" I told him what happened. The next day, someone from that indie label walked into my office with three dozen long-stem roses, and said, "I didn't know."

I guess he didn't know that I had some intense guardian angels. You had to know who your people were. Like John Brown was my brother, and he was with me, *always.* Until he passed. There were just people (and it wasn't just radio, it was records too), you had to know who-was-who, and who would have your back and who would not. Like when they let me go at Motown, Steve McKeever called and said, "I didn't know, what do you need? I was going in to talk to Jheryl…" I said, "I don't need anything right now." Because once it happened, I breathed a sigh of relief. Like this was not supposed to be for me. It wasn't. I had to contend to jealousies, that I had never, ever, ever, ever encountered before in my career. The atmosphere is like, "Okay, let me go." The funny thing was I didn't immediately get on a plane and go back to New York. I stayed in LA a little while longer. Then I came back to New York, but it was an experience. But through all of it, I made some lifelong friends, and had some experiences that other people don't get to have. I travelled extensively. It was wonderful.

One of my greatest champions was Bob Law. He has been there throughout my career, whether I was at the radio station or at the record company. If I needed anything I could call him, definitely. And Sylvia Rhone.

When I came back from LA after Motown I quit the industry. I went to work for Harlem Dowling. My girlfriend Toy, who is a makeup artist, but her and her husband were on the board, they were looking for someone for Communications. I went to work with them, because I thought I could help make a difference and bring attention to Harlem Dowling. I brought a lot of skills from the music industry to my job. One of the things that Ken Reynolds use to always say was, "I'm calling you, because I know, you're one of the people who reads newspapers. You're one of the people who really writes." Because a lot of us in key positions, would hire people to do the writing. But I always did my own writing.

I only stayed at Harlem Dowling for a year because it wasn't for me. But when you looked at those babies, the babies are what kept me there to begin with. The organization started out as an orphanage. Then they grew out of that into a social services for young people. It was on 125th Street and 7th Avenue. That was one of the things that made me crazy because I didn't want to travel up to Harlem every day from Jersey, but I did. It was in the building that was the old Hotel Theresa. I kind of loved it initially, and then I just came in one day and said, "I can't do this anymore." I sat in my office, because they had a thing for belittling people, and my assistant there told everyone about my resignation letter which said, "I don't need anybody here to define me, I already know who I am. I came here because I thought I could bring something to this situation, but you can't belittle me." They wanted me to punch a time clock! Like are you kidding me? I was horrified, and that really was the last straw! I am a director, and I'm punching a time clock? I don't think so.

Eventually, I went to work with an independent label, but it was hard. It was really a guy thing, and I got tired. So, I began to do some writing, and I did a lot of freelance stuff. Finally, I went to work for Hinton Battle because he was a good friend, and I knew he was trying to establish a Theater School and he had produced some independent plays. We worked together for quite a while at his offices on 42nd Street. He went to work on a movie on the West Cost, and I ran the office in New York. But it was difficult to get the cash flow, and many other things.

I could feel myself getting physically tired too. One day, I was walking down the street and I flipped down to the ground. I thought, *What the heck is going on?* It was difficult for me to get up, and when I did get up all I remember was that it was my daughter's 40th birthday. I went to her birthday party, and I could not walk up the stairs. I had developed a herniated disk that was compressing my spinal cord and my condition got worse, and worse, and worse.

When I was finally diagnosed, I had surgery and spent three months in Rehab. I went from a wheelchair to being able to walk with help now. I know I'm blessed with my health, and with the greatest accomplishment of having raised a beautiful my daughter.

There are a lot of artists I see today that make me feel good and bring back memories. I have really, really, really good memories. There are always folks who make me smile. Like watching that *New Edition Story!* Just look at these children, look at them! The thing that it made me think about was that, when I first started at Motown, I couldn't keep Michael Bivins out of my office. I'd ask him, "Well, what do you want now?" He truly wanted to know everything about the industry. *Everything*. He was just starting to build Biv Ten with all his little artists, so he really wanted to learn, it was not a joke for him., When I watch that *New Edition Story* I think, "Look at the babies!"

I'm not sure if I feel any kind of way because they never ever mention us women. Then there are a lot of times the artists are not necessarily responsible for that. It's the people who knew better like the heads of the record labels. The women are not an exclamation point, we're kind of like a comma. Honestly, I am OK about not being mentioned because I didn't have that kind of expectation.

The industry is totally different now, because the radio and records that we were a part of the entertainment industry is nonexistent. I would say to industry seekers… Do what inspires you. Do what you're passionate about. Don't allow anybody to tell you that you can't.

I would tell my younger self a lot of the stuff! How I entered the industry was accidental because I was going to be an actress. Working at a radio station was a detour that I didn't think was going to last. It was something I became passionate about, and then going into records was never my intention. I liked it, and I had a ball! I *had* a ball. I would tell my younger self, "Okay, follow your passions! Do what you want to do! Just don't get stuck behind a counter at Macy's."

Linda Haynes with After 7

Mic Check 15

"All Is Never Lost"

~by~

Alita Carter

I fell in love with music from the cradle and don't have a recollection of not ever loving music. It honestly is my religion. The vibration, sounds, power, and energy I receive from every note whether by instrument or through vocals is soul-stirring and as powerful as the ocean, wind, moon, and stars. I hear God.

The first Hip Hop song I ever heard was the Sugar Hill Gang's "Rapper's Delight" and though I was blown away, it was Whodini's "Five Minutes of Funk" that lives on my playlist some thirty years later. When I heard the beat, I was at full attention. Back in the day, it meant coming home from school, turning on the television, running into the kitchen, fixing a peanut butter and jelly sandwich, pouring a glass of milk, and the first instrumental chords dropped on 'Five Minutes of Funk'...I knew it was Video Music Box time.

Polygram /Mercury—Palm Tree Studios—Krush Rap TV—Source Magazine—Rap Pages Internships, Office Assistant, Director, Producer, Writer 1987, 1989, 1990

My start in the industry began with a series of internships coming out of Woodlands High School and into college. As a high school senior, I participated in a work-study program at my high school called W.I.S.E. that allowed students to obtain an internship during the second part of their graduating year. I landed a spot at New York's WPIX-TV Emmy-Award winning show "Best Talk", executive produced by the late Kathy Shearer-Shepherd, an alumnus of my high school and one of the highest ranking African American women in television at the time.

During my freshman year of college, I returned back to New York from Virginia with the quickness and met the infectious Tuffy Questell on the campus of Bronx Community College. He was a singer, host, and all around-great guy. I didn't know at the time he was affiliated with the show Video Music Box and his sister was one of the producers. We were talking about my background, and I told him about my internship at WPIX. He was wrapping up an internship at Polygram Mercury Records and wanted to know if I was interested because he wanted to make sure they had someone that could really rely upon.

My first music internship started at Polygram Mercury working in Publicity for Beverly Paige, VP of Publicity (Black Music), who would later become a great mentor into the business. In addition to meeting Beverly, I worked closely with her assistant Brenda Edwards, these ladies became my industry mothers. I witnessed the strength and creative genius they presented setting up the marketplace for acts like Kurtis Blow, The Fat Boys, Tony, Toni, Tone, Vanessa Williams, Nia Peoples, and Angela Winbush to name a few. I was surrounded by other great women like A&R Director Vivian Scott-Chew, and Jocelyn

Cooper, although an assistant at the time, was on her way to becoming an executive force in the next few years.

Beverly tapped into my writing and although an intern, I was paid to write captions for photos going to publications. She also began honing my skills as a biographer and I began writing and being paid to write artist bios.

While serving as an intern at Polygram, I was introduced to and later hired as an office assistant by Van Gibbs (Dad to super producer Salami Remi) to help manage the Palm Tree Recording Studios all the while being a full time college student and working part-time at a bookstore in Harlem. The things you do when you're young.

Through Van I began working with acts like Philly's MC Rell, and New York's Chuck Chillout and Kool Chip. In addition, Palm Tree Recording began renting production office space to Video Music Box so the exposure to Hip Hop increased exponentially. Between Palm Tree's recording studios and Video Music Box, it served as an incubator for talent like Director Hype Williams who was also fresh, young, and aspiring like me.

My exposure brought me in contact with people like Mike Elliot (Brown Sugar, Like Mike, Source Awards) who was from Philadelphia and producing a syndicated rap show similar to Video Music Box for the Philadelphia Tri-State area called Krush TV. He said he needed a producer/director and although I knew none of what that meant, we began filming interviews in Manhattan and airing them in Philly. Even though I got a bounced check...the show was supposedly syndicated in 21 markets within its first two years. We interviewed everyone from Gang Star, Main Source, MC Lyte, MC Serch, EST, Tribe and so many others.

Mike Elliot was young, determined and misguided initially, years later in 1992, while at Atlantic Records, I received a call from David Mayes (*Source* Magazine) wanting to know if I was willing to give Mike a job referral. Allowing bygones to be bygones, I chalked up whatever the math was or wasn't. It was not worth saying anything disparaging or throwing salt. The music business by that time had taught me we all can use another chance to make things right.

Somewhere in between I worked on another Hip Hop dance show being taped out of the Cotton Club, it was a blur and lasted about that long. In the meanwhile, I redirected my focus on school and by that time was writing for *The Paper* (City College of New York), *Rap Pages* and special interest projects with *The Source* Magazine. The writing and bios kept me in the business while I put more time into completing my studies.

Untouchables - Atlantic Records- Mecca Don—Universal Records
Production Coordinator, A&R Assistant, A&R Admin
A&R Director, Publishing Director
1992 - 1998

It was 1992 and by the time of graduation, I was a little nervous about where I would be working. Sharing my anxiety with Brenda Edwards (Polygram/Island) she introduced me to Dice Ramdanny, who instructed me to come down to The Untouchables office because they needed an intern in Publicity. Within minutes, Eddie F of Heavy D and The Boyz offered me an internship with this music production company. The last thing I wanted to do was another internship, but I knew better than anyone how quickly an internship could go from working for free to having a job. So, I reluctantly took the role assisting the PR Director Kim Lumpkin. It was about a week before Kim left Untouchables and went to Atlanta where she ultimately got onboard with LaFace Records and their successful roster.

Meanwhile I was promoted within days to PR Director, but that lasted about three days when I was informed that a Production Director was most needed given it was a production company. Not sure why that role became available, but it's the position which thrust me into the recording and production side of the business.

After spending all night reading files, studying licensing with ASCAP, BMI, SESAC and others, I had to familiarize myself with the publishing deal Untouchables had with Warner Chappell. To my relief, Jocelyn Cooper was THE woman in music publishing, so fortunately for me, I learned what I needed to just function until it all sank in.

This role put me at the beginning stages of producing a record. I discovered how much I loved the recording process - the studio, the songwriters, the engineers, musicians, and backup singers. It was the purest and most passionate part of the entire process because no one really knew where any song was going. It was the hope each time that a HIT was made, that others would hear what we were hearing in the studio.

After working with Eddie F, Pete Rock, David Hall, Nevelle Hodge and songwriters Eric Milter and the late Kenny Greene (original member of INTRO) who produced the music and sounds for the hottest albums and remixes during that time, I moved on quickly to Atlantic Records.

Throughout my career, there has always been someone from my home in the Greenburgh—White Plains area, a quiet suburban community less than 30 miles north of NYC, that has served as the catalyst for many of my next steps. My childhood sister-friend Jennifer Perry called me one day and told me her boy Benny Pough (Motown) who was from White Plains, might be able to help me as I was looking for work at the time. Benny basically hooked me up with his former boss and head of A&R at Motown who was becoming the new Sr. VP of A&R Black Music at Atlantic Records.

That meeting led me to a job as an A&R Assistant to Timmy Regisford (also House DJ for WBLS) at Atlantic Records for the next four years, allowing me to meet some of the most dynamic women and friends for life. Because we were under the auspice of Sylvia Rhone who left to run East West Records upstairs. Our division was clearly ruled by a strong, dynamic, and fierce Black woman who protected us, but just don't get outta line. That was the first lesson you learned at the gate!

Midway through my time at Atlantic, Timmy accepted a job at Dreamworks and I had a major family loss and I needed to take some time away from the work. In truth there wasn't any position I wanted in Black Music at the time and given the grief I was suffering, I was able to take time-off, collect unemployment, and rollerblade in Prospect Park all summer.

While on my "hiatus" I began working with Max Gouse and his cousin Roget Romain as they were launching Mecca Don Records as Director of Production managing their producers and administering the recordings. We released Adina Howard "Freak Like Me" as the first single and with the whole West Coast Dr. Dre Snoop sound being hot, Adina's record went Gold really fast. Sadly, as talented as she truly is, I was always concerned that her career would be ruined after the release of that song.

It wasn't long after that I got a call from Atlantic Records Legal and Business Affairs to join their division as an A&R Admin Coordinator. Having carefully managed the recording budgets for the Black Music Department in the past and the need to get someone that understood the process, created an opportunity for me.

Initially I felt isolated from the folk in the Black Music Division downstairs as I was now upstairs, with no color on our side of the building. Different, was an understatement. Overall, I learned what deals were being considered, what everyone was spending, the royalty checks that artist weren't collecting, and all things financial as it related to the recording process. On a few occasions I was called into a room full of White men trying to decide whether to give a label deal or production deal to some Hip Hop or R&B producer unknown by them. My Black-ness, Hip-Hop-ness, and Woman-prowess was called in as authority to help people without a clue.

I will say this, I watched plenty of paper go out the window on whack deals consigned by label friends and "silent" partners... A hellava lot of money was wasted, which is in part why a Black Music Division doesn't exist today. As an unapologetic conspiracy theorist, I can't blame it on "them" or "the man" …but I can say 'the man' and "them" didn't handle their business properly.

By 1995, I was administering over 250 recording budgets on several Atlantic labels, imprints, and subsidiaries, it was around this time two situations were happening. One, I received a call from a Shandi Quildon, a producer I had befriended who produced a song for Atlantic when I was in the Black Music Division, asking if I was still managing producers and if I'd be interested in managing he and his production partner. I agreed to a meeting.

Two, Doug Morris left Atlantic Records, launching Rising Tide via Universal Records, which caused a major upset in the label and shift in personnel.

During that time of Rising Tide's construction and reconstruction, my friend Cheryl (formerly of Untouchables) asked me to join her, as she had a meeting at Universal Records with Kedar Massenburg, manager of D'Angelo at the time and president of the new imprint Kedar Entertainment. Cheryl worked for Kedar when he managed Stetsasonic years earlier, so she wanted to play some tracks and catch up. After being introduced to him, I sat quietly as the two of them continued with their meeting and me wondering why I was there in the first place.

After their meeting ended Kedar asked what work I did. I explained my background and that I was currently working with a few producers and worked full time as an A&R Administrator. Over the next few weeks, we kept in touch as he was structuring his label.

Meanwhile, I meet with Shandi and his partner, who turned out to be Chico Debarge, younger brother in the Debarge legacy. At the time, Chico had just did a little over five years of federal prison time and had a plethora of songs he'd written with his boy while locked up. He and Shandi were producing songs and needed to place many of the tracks.

At the time, Chico had a recording contract with LaFace Records. He'd only been home for less than a year before Babyface signed him to the imprint. Although on the label, Babyface was unable to work with him because he was desperately trying to finish the Waiting to Exhale soundtrack. So, Chico's album on and off hold with various A&R people, who I knew were exploiting the budget with music never to be heard.

With the permission of his manager Fred Moultrie, who was also managing Chante' Moore at the time, we agreed that I would work on Chico's behalf as a producer and songwriter only. There was never any intent on my part to do any artist management. As luck would have it, Kedar really needed help managing the production and admin side of the recordings. Eventually I took a consultant position with Kedar Entertainment to manage that aspect of their label, while maintaining my position at Atlantic Records.

By this time, I had begun shopping Shandi and Chico's tracks to respective A&R people. Kedar heard a few of the songs and bought for two of his acts, one being Erykah Badu. As our business became more intertwined, we decided to merge managements and came with an agreement where I would shop his producers along with mine.

Since Chico was already signed to Laface, we weren't really looking for another recording deal, in all fairness and respect for Babyface, Chico was patiently waiting for Babyface's schedule to clear. Chico was fine writing and producing, which he loved more than singing. However, after a trip to LA meeting with his manager and Babyface, it was determined the direction Chico wanted to pursue and Face willing to give him a release amicably to not hold him back was agreed upon. So that left me.

While I was able to work with Kedar to get Chico a Demo Deal, we began fixing the songs Chico recorded earlier at home in a makeshift studio. Ultimately Chico was offered a recording contract with Kedar Entertainment after we used the demo deal to improve many of the initial recordings. During the same time, I'd left Atlantic Records and joined Kedar Entertainment full time to serve as A&R Director, eventually taking on the role of Publishing Director as well. We did ink a publishing deal with Sony with Erykah Badu and Chico Debarge in tow.

The Wonder Years (Digital Age)
Manager, A&R, Content Manager, Communities Producer, Partner, and Producer
Micah 7 Management, Kedar Ent, DME (Digital Mafia), BET.com, NuDawn Marketing
1997, 1998, 1999, 2000, 2001

The internet was amazing to me. I could pull up information across the country at any time, saving a trip to the library. I knew while sitting in my office that this technology was about to change EVERYTHING. I was able to see what was happening in other areas before sending an artist into a market.

Sadly, "peace" don't last always, especially in the music business. Rest assured when money is being made, egos are getting bigger. The same people you helped to get to "the promised land" are no longer needing insight and intellect; they are now surrounded by 'Yes' men and woman who water their ever-growing inner celebrity.

In my final year as an A&R Director was dramatic and filled with personal issues, backstabbing, intimidation and daily harassment. Even though I was going into Universal, I was also running my management company Micah 7. I was managing recording engineers, a few producers, aspiring filmmakers, and of course one artist. But things change. And I was ready for change.

Honestly, I was young and not business savvy enough to manage the environment. Once the industry became more thugged-out and I'm seeing bodyguards sitting outside of executive's offices... And after every album launch party where I found myself running from bullets, I knew it was time to make a change. Yes, I left and went into Technology into the wonderful world wide web.

I was a creative and artist to some degree myself, so business wasn't always managed so well for me. I was great for my clients but neglected my own affairs. I eventually folded Micah 7 and joined Darrien Dash with his Digital Mafia Enterprises. Of course, I thought the name was so very hood and told him to just call it "DME" especially if it was about to become a public company on the NY Stock exchange. I worked there providing content and layout for websites we were building for various companies and artists. At the time to get someone to build a website was like buying a house. It was all this fancy jargon these companies didn't understand so they shelled out big money to ensure their presence was on the World Wide Web. Crazy.

I didn't stay at DME long after a few bounced checks and late payments, I began looking for work and that wasn't easy. However, the internet helped me locate a position at BET in their new digital space. At the time I had no choice but to take an Employment Training position with the NY Social Security Unemployment office getting people ready for the job world through the Welfare to Work program. Crazy x Crazy.

Here I am training people who were being forced off welfare and not open to the training and I was miserable training them. That lasted all of two weeks before I received a call to move to Washington DC and join the BET.com team in launching the networks first site. WHEW!!!

I moved to DC, keeping my apartment in Hackensack—renting it out to Universal while India Aire recorded her album. I was now a Communities Producer. How appropriate.

After launching the communities' pages for BET.com, I became very aware of all the activities happening throughout the country. I also traveled to all the national conventions (NAACP, Urban League, Delta Sigma Theta, Alpha Kappa Alpha) promoting the brand and trying to close the "digital divide" signing up over 100,000 people to provide email addresses.

After several months of no sleep, working until 1AM, I received a raise, a great job evaluation and stock options. Then two weeks later I was fired. Crazy x Three. Yes, a crazy boss who was very intimidated. Never understood the motive. Years later a VP with the company revealed that her intimidation led her to come in an executive meeting with the COO crying profusely about how I said the most awful things to her regarding her infertility, and marriage. Even Crazier, I never ever knew she had problems with either. To my understanding we had a good relationship. I received an apology from this former VP for being roped into believing this woman's nonsense and comforting her through her crocodile tears. All wasn't lost.

It's Show Time
Showtime Networks
2001-2005

At this point serving as a Production Coordinator for Showtime Champion Boxing and ShoBOX brought me not only back to television but to LIVE and Pay-per-View. Forced to work under the constraints of making absolutely no mistakes. With LIVE, there is no room. In addition, it was a male dominated arena, so any weakness that could be attributed to you being a woman, would definitely be said.

A long way from music, television brought me up to speed on execution and delivery. Although a creative environment, television didn't have the wait time as the music industry. Things had to be done and waiting on clearances for music from record labels or music publishing companies, forced television into working directly with independent label and music sources. I was told I could stay at ShowTime Boxing my entire life, but the promise of promotion was slim given the boys club and people maintaining their positions. Even though I applied for other areas of Viacom, my division VP would have to approve. I learned that it was blocked several times since they considered me a valuable person on their team, I was denied the opportunity to grow in that network. So, I left.

Strictly Business and Strictly Independent
2005—Today

My education was basically on the job training. My degree course work wasn't related to the any of the work, but the analytical discernment skills used in logic, strategy and research in an academic environment proved beneficial and necessary when dealing with some many aspects of the music business. But the true Rockstar moment, is when you're standing in a room with your peers and the love is just so real. The validation from *them* is absolutely EVERYTHING!

It was indeed a boys' world. Many of the guys were cool, supportive and became your brothers and friends for life; but it also was a big extended college campus, so sexual harassment was a normal thing. Lines were crossed religiously. As a woman I worked harder, kept the balls rolling and juggled in the air, but was often paid less, cheated out of promotions or album credits. As a Black woman I was expected to "look out for a brotha," and being a nurturer, I confused family/friend camaraderie with business dealings. When it came down to it, I know as women we had to help each other because the men were very selfish. Once you helped them over the threshold, they forgot how the splits, credits, and new deals that *you* set up were supposed to benefit you.

Sadly, I'm so numb to the omission of women in the documentaries and biopics, that I have to separate my mind just to be able to enjoy the story. Deep down I and others like me remain in the shadows as mere props in a history so deep, that we all know there can never be His-story without Her-story. At no time in the world can it ever be. Hip-Hop would certainly be Hip-NOT!!

I would give the young ladies a "scared straight" type conversation. This business is rewarding, but not for the faint of heart. You will be excited and scared at the same time…maybe even all the time. That some girls do…and some girls don't but knowing who you are and being authentic will take you further with honey than with salt.

My post-entertainment industry life took me through worlds of finance, pharmaceutical, government and currently expanding in real estate development. Having transitioned my career several times over, I'm proud of my recent works as a director of a community center; redirecting it into a cultural epi-center providing arts & culture, serving seven years as a program director managing a successful city-wide nutrition grant program, becoming a "Vision Enabler" and author of

"Framing Our Visions, partnering in a print-media publishing company, developing and trademarking a granola called "Blaqola"; dedicated to supporting Black artist and the beat goes on...

With so many opportunities in sight, all my lights are on green.

"...Oooh watch me, watch me..." Dance and all.

Mic Check 16

"Play Your Soundtrack"

~by~

Tracey Moore

Music was the soundtrack of my life. I grew up in a household where I was the only girl and the middle child. My mother, it was a generation where they just did not talk to you, and children really were seen and not heard. Children did not participate in adult conversations, so I literally learned about sexual education through the book *Are You There God? It's Me, Margaret.*

For me, Earth, Wind & Fire was my freedom. Earth, Wind & Fire was like a living bible to me. I also loved school and I did very well in school. I went to Catholic school, but not everybody liked me. I grew up with some bullies, and I would get bullied every day. *Everyday.* I was tall too, like 5'4" in first grade wearing a size nine shoe. To this day, Caroll and I are still best friends after fifty years to this day. We were the big ones, so that's how we became friends because we were the same size.

We were always teased, and they used to call me sasquatch, Spacey Tracey, and Loosey. Instead of taking it in and allowing it to destroy my Spirit, I flipped it and I made fun of it too and became a class clown. That led me into acting.

It was a defense mechanism, and when I came home, my freedom was music and to listen to Earth, Wind & Fire singing "*Keep your head to the sky!*" Gladys Knight taught me love, with songs like "Neither One of Us" and "Best Thing That's Ever Happened to Me" and Chaka Khan. There were words that were spoken in the 70s, that were lessons. I remember Jeffrey Osborne's "Love Ballad" and I thought, *I don't know what's going on with me or what I'm feeling... but wow! I want to feel this all the time!*

Then my dad loved Jazz. I'm talking about Miles Davis, Sarah Vaughan. Music was always played in our house. We always had a turntable, and we always had a radio. For me, that was my freedom. Then I also believe I was definitely creating music videos when I was six years old. When I would get in trouble or if I couldn't talk to my mother I would go in my room, play a record, and close my eyes and just imagine scenes with the music. I did it with everything!

My mother was extremely negative growing up, and now looking back that was her ammunition to push us, but we didn't get the love and the support or the balance from that. It was always just push, push, push. I would go to my room and listen to Gladys Knight & The Pips and I'd think, *Yes, I'm going to be okay!* The comedy is that, when my daughter Radiance was growing up, I used to teach her about life through music. Once when she was upset that kids were talking about her and teasing her I said, "They smile in your face all the time they want to take your place! They're backstabbers, but you were raised not knowing anything but to feel empowered."

So when I was taking her to Howard for her first year, and then we heard that song she asked, "You taught me from songs?!?" I extracted things from *The Wiz* "Home". That's how I would teach, and when she caught onto that it was hilarious! That music was the key in my life!

After I graduated from Mercy High School in San Francisco I was accepted to the Pacific Conservatory of the Performing Arts in

Santa Maria, California. I had a really strict schedule, from eight in the morning until sometimes one or two in the morning because allegedly first-year students couldn't perform so we had to help out with the production. I got fired from everything basically, there were a series of mishaps including breaking a sewing machine.

I was there with Dorien Wilson, who is now a working actor. Dorien and I were the only people of color, and it was so challenging because we constantly heard that we didn't sound Black, but we were always cast for the Black roles. I grew up in the late 60s, the Black Panthers era, and my parents used to say "Say It Loud, I'm Black and I'm Proud." So basically, I always had something to say. At any given time a teacher would say, "Tracey Moore go sit outside" and let me cool off. I got pneumonia late in that year, and my dad came to take me home. I didn't come back, and they all called me. They called me and Dorien called me because I had gotten cast in *Grease* for the Chita Rivera character. They really wanted me to go back, but it wasn't a great experience fighting what I call today racism. I didn't have the fight in me because I didn't have the fight to become an actor. I was just studying because I wanted to be a director. I figured that would be a good place for me to start, and to be able to understand and communicate with the actors.

In 1983 I moved to New York from San Francisco at the cusp of Rap, not knowing it. I met Steve Salem in the studio with Run DMC, and they asked me, "Do you know rap?"

I said, "Yeah, there's the Sugarhill Gang."

They shouted, "That's not rap!" I thought, *Oh, my God, it's so aggressive here in New York.* At a very young age, I married Steve Salem who was partners initially with Russell Simmons and managing Run DMC, Houdini, and Full Force. He had an allegiance with Bowlegged Lou because they went to Syracuse University together, and they were best friends.

I was 22 with a young child, my husband was always in the studio, always on the road, and always somewhere. So, for the first two years of my daughter's life I was stable, but I did not have any friends. I had to make my life. I remember my time in Brooklyn and looking outside of the brownstone window hearing "Changed" in the background thinking, *Tracey, it's going to be okay.* Whatever those songs were during those times were my inspiration, and that's how I moved. Because I in New York by myself with no family and friends, the Walter Hawkins and Tramaine Hawkins song "Changed" was my mantra. Gospel music got me through the times when I didn't think I was going to get through. I'll never walk away from music, because that's the soundtrack of my life. In my acting classes, one of the homework assignments is to write all of the songs that comprise the soundtrack of your life. Yeah, you need to know that because sometimes you have to play your soundtrack to get through tough times in life.

My first job in the industry was casting a music video by the group Hi-Five. Lionel Martin was the director, and Darrin Henson was the choreographer. I loved the people I was working around, but I did not love the world of music videos at that time because it was unknown territory, but there was *a lot* of money. Music videos were literally 24-hour day shoots, and it wasn't about talent. There was no reading of sides - which are pages of a script - it was mainly girls walking around in revealing clothes. I felt like there was something wrong in that. I was very anxious to get out. I count the music videos, but I really count *Just Another Girl on the I-R-T*, as my first major project in film the industry. It started opening the doors for more work. The movie has become a classic and recently celebrated its 25th anniversary!

My position in the industry from 1987-2000…well I would say still to present day, just not as active, was as a Casting Director. A Casting Director is a liaison between the director and the talent. We merge the two together, but we don't make the final decision. We strongly suggest, and highly recommend, and begged and pleaded for good talent sometimes. I worked in film, television, and commercials. I started out with music videos, but I mainly lived in television and film.

Around 1988 or 1989 I was working for MTVs comedy show, called the *Boston Comedy Club* in The Village in New York. My favorite part of it was the scouting. They would give me a camera person, and we could go to any club for free. They treated us like royalty because they knew when I showed up that MTV was there. This kid comes on stage and I'm thinking, *Oh. My. God. This is it*! He was eighteen or nineteen and AWESOME! They wanted to develop the show *TRL,* with a comedian as host. I was auditioning every White comedian from Dave Attell to Kevin James and his brother. <u>All</u> of these White cats that are working now. So, I decided I was going to bring in this young Black kid, even if they were looking for a White guy. It was my first time really trusting my instincts, because I was still young in the game and learning. I brought the young man in front of my producer, Ted Demme, Joe Stolerman (who runs Hulu now). It was Dave Chappelle. They passed on him.

Two or three years later, after Dave's performance in *Robin Hood in Tights* it was clear that they had slept on him. I get a show to cast at MTV and they asked me, "Tracey, can you get that Dave Chappelle guy?"

I said, "No." MTV had the opportunity to hire him, and they knew he was the first person that I had literally found and brought in to cast. To this day, Dave and I are friends. When I see him there is a gratitude, he tells me how I helped him so much.

I worked with Lionel Martin and Ralph McDaniels, they had classic concepts with their production company, and they turned out two to three videos a week! One week I casted videos for R. Kelly,

Public Announcement, The Barrio Boys, and Keith Sweat. I would audition on a Saturday, and with the overflow, I would just call those people all the time. I would build my files so that we had "viddy hoes," (back in that time this was the terminology.) They had close to million-dollar budgets and Lionel Martin became a golden child, and artists like Boyz II Men, SWV, Jodeci *had* to be directed by Lionel Martin. I came up with Hype Williams, who was an art director turned director. All of these guys successfully transitioned to film and TV.

I got my first big break casting for film with *New Jersey Drive* because Spike Lee was the executive producer, Nick Gomez was the director who was on the come up. This was a time of independent film when it was ripe, and by any means necessary people would get their film done. Whether it was Maddie Rich with credit cards or John Singleton mortgaging his house to get his film done. There were not crowdfunded opportunities back then, so directors would borrow from family and friends. But after *She's Gotta Have It*, there was this fever of I-can-get-a-film-done-and-I-don't-even-have-a-Hollywood-budget mentality.

So, *New Jersey Drive* was a film originally cast by Todd Baylor and this is when I started out as a casting director. I didn't know anything about being a Casting Director, I just knew that I knew a lot of actors, and I could help them get work. I called five Casting Directors from the Ross Report - which was just the directory - and I called Todd Baylor. All of the casting directors either hung up on me or they just didn't give me any information. Then I called them saying 'I was a student at NYU writing about how underrated casting directors were.' Then I started to get information. But the irony was that Todd Baylor got fired from *New Jersey Drive* and I got replaced to Casting Director. I used to go with him to get his notes and his files, I reminded him of this story. He didn't remember, but he said, "Wow, I should've taken the time to at least give you some information." He thanked me for pointing that out.

When the TV series *New York Undercover* became super-hot I was casting the music artists to perform and extras for the club scene at the end of the show. Natalie's was the club on the show that I would cast all of the actors in. I was the extras casting director, so I had the regulars that I would cast all the time and one of my extras was Jane Rosenthal's mom, who was Robert De Niro's partner. It was just so crazy how one day she said she wanted to introduce me to her daughter Jane, and I put the two words in my mouth, "Jane… Rosenthal?" We actually had a meeting in Tribeca, and it was wonderful.

At Natalie's I had to cast the waitresses and the staff and then also the crowd. I can't remember the first group we had but Andre Harrell had a heavy affiliation with the music industry so he tapped into the Uptown artists first. Then once we got Mary J. Blige, everyone wanted to be on the show. It got to the point where we literally had a waiting list of people and we had to tell A-List artists, "Okay, next show! Or we're going to get you on." It grew into something big, and it really was this idea of having this separate club where the characters Malik and Michael would always end their day.

The artists I booked were considered the top artists of the time. I started coaching because I noticed a discomfort in people just even being themselves. Although these artists were portraying themselves, it was evident that they were uncomfortable in front of a camera and that was another reason why I started coaching.

I hadn't started teaching officially, but I would give them advice. Some of them to this day come back to say, "Tracey, you gave me some really good advice, have you ever thought about teaching people?" Then they used to always ask me in auditions if I taught, and it wasn't until 1996 that I started teaching. I was still casting but that's when I made the decision to try one class. I had three people at first, and then I was blessed to having a waiting list. I had a celebrity in every class, and I always wanted the other actors to feel like they were all on the same playing field…because they were.

As an acting coach, I've been with Busta Rhymes for more than 20 years, so I would definitely consider him my pet project. I was on the road with him for six years consistently, from Steve Harvey to Shaft, to all of the roles he did. I was on the road as his acting coach for every show, film, and television project that he did, and I lived with him. And as an acting coach, if need be, I would travel with my clients. Specifically, for six years I travelled with Busta Rhymes and Eve on all of their projects. I would live in hotels, they had accessibility to me on the set, from the call time to wrap time. Sometimes in their hotel rooms we would go over lines and that became a job for me for six years, and it grew from me just being an acting coach to really being a consultant in their TV and film careers. I read every script, and I would have to regurgitate that back to them because they didn't have time to read a script. So, I went from being an acting coach to being personally invited to every meeting out in LA with the "powers-to-be," like producers and studio heads to give my input.

Speaking of myself and Busta Rhymes because he's not an easy person to work with. He very much knows what he wants, and he very much speaks his mind, but I found a place in his Spirit. To this day, we still have this crazy, crazy connection where I will say to myself, *I love Busta Rhymes, and I can't love Busta Rhymes anymore.* But then something happens, and we witness how our love has grown even more for each other. We are strictly platonic, and he trusts me implicitly because he knows that I have his best interest at heart, and as difficult as it may be to disagree with him I will stand my ground and do just that. I always felt like I was the grown one among the entourage. So, I wasn't making decisions based on being a favorite, or trying to stand out, I was making decisions based on honesty.

After we worked on *Finding Forrester* with Sean Connery and Gus Van Sant that opened the doors for Busta to be the actor or musical artist that white A-and B-list actors wanted to buddy up with. The thing that hindered us was during that time, he did not want to cut his locks. That's where things would get a little tricky, because not every character had dreadlocks. He finally cut them around 20 years ago because I cut mine first, and then like three years later he cut his.

I feel that my greatest area of strength in my work is that I authentically and legitimately care about people. That is a huge plus, but it can also be a huge minus. I invest in people from day one, and if they believe then I believe. For me, that's been the fuel. Being a Casting Director all of these years it's a very, very monotonous job. It can get tedious, draining, and straining because it is a lot of work. The thing that kept me alive was every day, was when I was auditioning and someone walked into the room, I'd think that person is going to be huge. I also love actors, so I never got bored.

True story...I was working on *Kiss of Death* and Morgan Spurlock was a production assistant. I didn't know him, but I was friends with his friend Ray who was the production manager. I was also working on a Sony project on the side They wanted to cast a comedian to travel across the United States and introduce new Sony equipment. They specifically wanted a comedian, someone with some charm. They were paying them $3,500 a week for a year. Morgan, at that time, was making around $100-$125 a day but was not thriving in New York. I didn't know any of this. To this day, I don't know how Ray found out, but he did, and he came into my office because he heard about this Sony project and asked if his friend Morgan could audition. I said yeah sure, and so Morgan auditioned, and they loved him. I started coaching him, not knowing whom I was coaching, and I told him they really like you. Morgan gets the job, and he went from doing that to developing relationships within Sony where he started directing industrial films then leading to *Super Size Me.* People will call me, as in White people, to tell me that Morgan Spurlock mentioned my name on CNN!

After *Super Size Me*, Morgan took me to lunch and he said, "I need to tell you the real story." He said that he was originally going to move to West Virginia, give up on his career, and that job saved his life. He said, "Tracey, I went from $150 at a point where I was barely eating, barely living, to $3,500 a week. You changed my life." Our relationship flourished from there.

There are certain things that are hard about this industry, but being a woman can literally feel like the challenges are levitating. There are women in the industry who take on this armor. One literally came up to me her first day of shooting and said, "Tracey, do you know why I wear pantsuits every day?" I said that I didn't.

She responded with, "Because I want men to look at me like a man, and not like a woman." For a woman to have to conjure up something that intense for protection and it doesn't matter if you're homosexual or heterosexual, is insane.

One situation that I had, coaching one of my artists, and after we were finished they asked, "Hey Tracey, we're going to go hang out, do you wanna go?"

I questioned, "Where are we going?"

They told me, "Don't ask questions let's just go."

So, I replied by saying that I'm married and have children and I like to know where I'm going. Finally, with a lot of resistance, they said they were going to the Cheetah Club to do Ecstasy. That's a Dominatrix club in LA. I said that I didn't know anything about Ecstasy and had never tried it, so I asked what it does.

They responded, "It makes you want to take your clothes off and basically sleep with everybody."

Not the drug for me... They told me fine and that they'd call me later. I never got a call. For about a week after that, I would walk up to them in the lobby after work and they would spread like roaches. I would literally walk up to them and ask how they were doing, and they would disperse. It wasn't until Kellita Smith (*The Bernie Mac Show*), who is a best friend of mine, told me that was a test. She said she had gone to a dinner with seven or eight of the top actresses in the industry, and they were saying the "in-thing" for that time was to go to a strip club and bring a stripper back to the house for you and your man. No thank you!

I realized I was rocking in my career when the CBS Early Morning Show did a piece on me. After that my phone started ringing with rap artists and I had new clients basically every other day. The rockstar was Davidson, and she represented Ludacris and had given me everybody that she had worked with except Ludacris. He was the golden child. After the CBS feature she called me up and said Ludacris wants to work with you, and I was like ummm... he knows me? This was back during *Law & Order* days.

I met him during one of the worst snowstorms in New York City. My babysitter had just canceled so I had to take my son Miles to the hotel at 59th Street all the way from Brooklyn. I was just barely able to make it. When I finally walk through the doors, Ludacris is like a fan and says, "Tracey, I'm so glad that you came!" He was so gracious and asked if Miles needed anything. In my head I thought, *Tracey do not show your expression*!

Then he says, "Tracey, I told Dana, that I refuse to get on any set unless I work with Tracey Moore."

I thought *really? You said that?*

I remember walking out of the hotel saying to myself... *I'm guess I'm a big deal. I'm not pursuing clients, but people are really calling me.*

Then Common contacted me, and when I could not meet him in person he asked me if we could coach on the phone. It was the first time I ever coached on a phone. I said to myself, *I'll just close my eyes and connect in some way.* I was able to do it, and that was a moment for me where I felt, *Okay, I must be a big deal.* And if Ludacris is specifically saying 'I'm not getting on this set.' That episode won an Emmy.

My biggest regret... I always say I have none, because the thing about regrets for me is you in some way or another are changing the course of history. I just feel my life is designed for everything to happen for a reason. As challenging as it was, you know I got a job at a furniture store when I first got to New York City making $125 a week, and my rent in Harlem with two other roommates was $95 a month. Sometimes my check didn't stretch, so maybe two days a week I had to walk from 145th Street and Amsterdam to 14th Street in Union Square. It was either food or transportation, and food always won.

The most important thing you need to know entering into the industry is to know yourself. It is a constant evolution of who you are going to be, but to know the foundation you stand on when you respect and love yourself. Teaching tangible tools young women can walk away with about them having value is something I think the Me Too movement has a responsibility to provide. We are not just sex symbols, fantasies, or anything else. Here is a fact, I have been in New York for more than 35 years and I have never, ever, ever had an incident.

In this industry our hours are not nine-to-five, and there were moments where I had to come home on the train at 2am by myself, so there were opportunities for things to happen. But I think that people know who they can mess with. I always wore an armor like I had an attitude when I was outside. I'm saying this to say there's a way to establish respect, and I have had to do it with the majority of my clients since they were men. These men always approached me from a standpoint of ma'am or Ms. Tracey, until I said call me Tracey, Ms. Moore is my mother.

Today, I co-host a series I created called *Inside the Black Box* along with Emmy-winning actor Joe Morton. On this show we share deep conversations, workshops, and discussions about the role race plays in the entertainment world with guests like Sherri Shepherd, Shonda Rhimes, Debbie Allen, and Ta-Nehisi Coates to name a few. As this creation pulled into the station to the soundtrack of my life, that although it was a long time coming, I am satisfied with the timing of its arrival.

Tracey Moore coached Cardi B on the film Hustler.

Mic Check 17

"Develop Your Game F.A.C.E."

~by~

Robin Dunn

"***Dancer's feet, movin' to the sounds of the underground. Backspins, headspins, scratchin' spinnin', graffiti art you don't wanna stop. 70's, 80's, 90's now. What happened to Hip Hop so different from its start?…*** "These words were inspired from my days performing as a background singer and dancer with The Fatback Band. That experience took my love for music and dance to another level entirely. Surrounded by musicians, singers, and production crews along with worldwide travel expanded my hunger for more.

I fell in love with both music and dance when I attended my first dance recital in Queens at The Charlotte Pollak Dance Studio and saw my childhood friend Janis Jasper perform in the studio recital. I immediately went home and asked my Mom if I could join the dance school and she said, "Sure baby." It was there I learned Ballet, Tap, and Jazz. I studied Jazz with Frank Hatchett at Jo Jo's Dance Factory (now Broadway Dance Center) and ultimately, Ballet, Horton, and Dunham techniques at Alvin Ailey.

I was later hired for my legal and administrative skills to work with famed entertainment attorney, Louise C. West followed by Principle Management, a management company ~~for~~ representing the rock band U2. My sisters and I formed Duntori & Company a full-service artist development and management company followed by my creating E. D. Entertainment, the home of my F.A.C.E. brand specializing in self-discovery, performance technique and movement.

Music provided the foundation of my existence from dance to recording to performing while providing a livelihood I never expected during my early years as an artist and choreographer.

With a bachelor's degree in Business Administration (Marketing Management) from Baruch College in New York City I was able to handle any business coming my way. Not only was I a dancer for the Fatback Band, I was also a background singer, and office manager.

Historically speaking, my sisters and I were the first to bring Hip Hop dance to mainstream studios. I have been a faculty member at Broadway Dance Center (1989-1994), Steps on Broadway (1999-Present), Hunter College Adjunct Professor 2008- 2014), Alvin Ailey (2003-Present), and most recently at The City College of New York teaching "Hip Hop Dance, History and Cultural Importance."

As a member of The Fatback Band my all-time favorite Hip Hop jam is "Gotta Get My Hands on Some (Money)" by The Fatback Band featuring King Tim III. It was the first commercial rap record; however, they rarely get the credit for it as most give that honor to The Sugar Hill Gang. My other Fatback favorite is the R&B classic, "I Found Lovin."

Some of the artists I have worked with are Missy Elliot, Chris Brown, Sean Kingston, Raven Symone, The Braxton's featuring Jay

Z, Wynonna Judd, Jennifer Holliday, Joe, Will Downing, Brian McKnight, and I am also the former Director of Amateur Night at the world famous Apollo Theater. I would say working with Joe was one of my favorite experiences as he encouraged and supported my creative ideas and process. He gave me total creative freedom.

As a woman in the industry, gaining respect from male colleagues at times when handling business and shopping deals was challenging to keep the focus on the business versus other agendas.

My faith comes first in everything I do in life. Since my Mom passed away in 2015, I tap into her spirit as well to help me with difficult situations. In my coaching I always encourage clients to create their own survival tools to aid with difficult moments. All that being said, when in difficult rooms I tap into all my survival tools and keep the energy flowing with confidence.

My Mom raised us to be leaders, to be exceptional. Being the first came natural to us. When my sisters and I created our company Duntori, it was the first of its kind. We had our challenges, yes, but persevered because as I mentioned we were raised to be the best, if not, among the best. To be first at something didn't intimidate us because it was part of our upbringing. In addition, we had a lot of support from others in the industry who wanted to see us win. One of my most awesome moments was joining U2 on stage at Madison Square Garden.

I have been able to overcome ~~any~~ challenges by maintaining my focus and keeping my eyes on the prize at all times. A strong family bond made all the difference and helped immensely during hard times. I pursued projects I wanted to work relentlessly!!! At Duntori, my sisters and I would say, "Have no shame." We just kept our eyes on our goals no matter what and didn't allow anyone to deter us. There were plenty of nay-sayers, but we kept going. There were many times I wanted to quit but I didn't because of my faith, and because of my support system. It helped so much to have each other. Something else my Mom instilled in us was, "Take care of each other."

I've been blessed with great mentors, and my first champion was my Mom Edith E. Dunn Others were: Charlotte Pollak (Dance Teacher), Bill Curtis (Fatback Band), Carole Sylvan (Recording Artist, Fatback Band/mentor), Louise West, Esq., Ellen Darst (U2), and Peter Casperson (The Invasion Group).

My greatest accomplishment is forming our family business Duntori & Company and working alongside my two sisters Desiree Dunn Crichlow and Greta Dunn.

My most embarrassing moment occurred with a wardrobe malfunction while performing with the Fatback Band at the world-famous Apollo Theater. My top didn't support me properly and similar to Janet, I experienced a wardrobe malfunction.

I feel a keen sense of accomplishment when I see artists who are still relevant today knowing I helped do that! When I hear their songs on the radio, it's a good feeling and confirmation I know what I'm doing and to keep going. So, when I see the women who worked hard behind the mic, I know my worth and contributions and I keep things moving to continue my own progress.

I would tell my younger self to be willing to change in a timely manner. Have your own development plan with a very specific timeline and financial plan. Knowing when to make a move is important. My sisters and I ended our business when the music industry changed to its current status. It became necessary for me to shift my focus from artist development and management to self-discovery, performance technique and movement.

As for navigating the industry today, I advise artists to be prepared and thoroughly trained in their craft. Be sure to secure a mentor, learn the business, and the financial aspect of your industry. Don't stop until you attain your goals. When dealing with tight situations, resist showing your emotions and stay focused on your goals. I am a passionate, emotional, and transparent person. It took time for me to develop my Game F.A.C.E. As I learned to keep my cool at all times, I learned to focus my energies on execution and results, verses passion and emotion. I've missed key opportunities when I allowed the latter to dominate my actions.

The most important survival skill I have found that I could not do without in the business is prayer. It is still number one on my list. What I miss the most about the industry is working with my sisters. We were a good team. My Mom always thought I should be on television. I regret this didn't happen before her passing.

Today I work as a F.A.C.E. Coach. F.A.C.E. is an acronym and self-created development technique which equals, Focus, Attitude, Confidence, Energy and Eye contact. I specialize in coaching private clientele with self-discovery, performance technique, and movement. I also serve as a Creative Director and produce my own events and productions. Additionally, I am a Hip Hop Instructor at the Alvin Ailey, and Steps on Broadway, and an Adjunct Professor at The City University of New York's City College.

One of my favorite quotes is, "a teacher's job is to shape lives, build dreams and give hope for the future." ~Author, Unknown

WAKEPRAYSLAY
REPEAT

Mic Check 18

"Learn Absolutely Everything"

~by~

Miko L. Mathews

When I was a kid, music was everything. My grandmother would sing around the house, and I learned to work the record player when I was three. Some of my fondest memories are playing Gladys Knight & The Pips and singing into the mic—spelled brush—"If I Were Your Woman…" As I got older, I would sing in choirs at church, and I taught myself harmony when I was 10 years old.

I first auditioned for band when I was in the sixth grade. I had my heart set on playing the flute, but the White band director told all of the Black girls that they couldn't play the flute because their lips were too big. I didn't join that year.

In Jr. High, I played the baritone horn, which was the brass instrument right below the tuba. I'm only 5'1 now, so you can imagine how little I was then with that huge instrument. I decided at that point that I HAD to learn how to play the flute because there was NO way I could march with that baritone in Texas heat. I got a coke bottle to learn embouchure and I got a drumstick and drew the keys on it to learn fingering. My new band director, who looked more like me, let me go to contest on the flute and I made a two—with one being the highest. Not bad for a self-taught musician!

Throughout high school, I sang in the choir—whether or not I was actually in the class. When I got to college, I thought I'd major in Radio/TV/Film but call of the music was much stronger.

My career path has been anything but traditional. My major was music with minors in behavioral analysis and sociology. (When people would ask me what I planned to do with that, I'd say, "Explore new levels of poverty because I'm clearly not poor enough now.")

As far as my singing career, I kinda gave it up. I came up in the era where Yolanda Adams and Kim Burrell were new to the scene, and the Kirk Franklin & The Family first album had just dropped. Inasmuch as I thought I had a good voice; I was completely intimidated by all the great singers in the Dallas-Fort Worth area. I decided that if I couldn't BE on the records, I would play them.

My mom, who was a teacher, used to do radio on the side. Once, when I was in college, she was working at a station, and I was hanging out with her. Someone didn't show up for work, and they put me on. The lady who put me on-the-air had a friend that later became Tom Joyner's personal assistant. I ended up interning with Tom in the fall of 1995, and I worked with Doug Banks.

Because I was at ABC Radio, there were all kinds of opportunities available. I worked in the clearance department, for *Radio Disney* as an on-air talent, for *The Touch* as the host of *The Saturday Night Jam Session* and the entertainment feature called *In Touch*, and as an on-air talent and producer for *Rejoice! Musical Soul Food.*

It was the *In Touch* feature that led me to New York City. Because I was writing and producing the show. I thought I would be a good editor and producer. When I saw the job listing, I gave them a call. When I told the lady who I was, the first thing out of her mouth was, "We're not hiring in the urban department." I was like, "Okay...but what does the job entail? She told me, and the reiterated her original point about it not being an urban position. I replied, "But if I can write, I can write." She had to concede that point. She ended up inviting me to New York to take a writing test, and they offered me a job before I left.

The way I got to SiriusXM was also non-traditional. The woman I'd worked with at *Rejoice*—Willie Mae McIver—was friends with Ty Murrell—the original format manager of the Kirk Franklin's Praise channel. They were discussing personalities, and Willie Mae told Ty, "Oh, Miko's up there. Give her a call." Next thing I knew, I started working there right after 9/11. In fact, my official start date is September 12, 2001.

I interned with *The Tom Joyner Morning Show* in fall 1995. I worked on *The Doug Banks Show* as an associate producer from 1996 to 1998. I was on Radio Disney in 1997. *The Saturday Night Jam Session* and *InTouch* on The Touch were from 1998-1999. I moved in New York City and worked for *ABC ePrep* from 1999-2006. After that, I moved to Los Angeles, where I worked as a writer for *The John Tesh Show* from 2010-2011, and as an associate producer and on-air talent for Playboy Radio from 2011 to 2013. I came back to New York City in 2013, and I've been an editor and producer for Dr. Dave's Ultimate Prep since then. Today I have been hosting the morning show for *Kirk*

Franklin's Praise on Sirius XM channel 46 since 2001 under the name "Gina Rodgers." I also served as the executive producer of *Rejoice! Musical Soul Food*'s remote broadcasts from 1999-2005.

It is a good thing that I am a people person, first, and foremost. I also have a healthy sense of humor and a quick wit. Finally, I am determined to do what I want to do. When I was in high school, I knew I didn't want to get pregnant and be stuck in my hometown of Jefferson, Texas. And once I knew I loved radio, I had to be in it. Period.

As quiet as it's kept, I was one of the first people to actually produce a remote broadcast in gospel. Because my background was secular radio, my way of handling things was more exacting. Gospel radio—back in 1999—was more go with the flow. Basically, they'd snatch up whomever was passing through be a guest. My method was to call the record companies to actually schedule people for specific timeslots. Of course, I met with a LOT of resistance.

I remember once one of the other networks was broadcasting next to us, and they'd just played a song by the artist I'd scheduled next. The producer came up to the artist to see if they come over and talk to them. I was like, "Nope…we have him scheduled. You can get him after." I know they were mad at me, but I didn't care. Several record reps had a problem with me, too. I have a tendency to be very direct with little use for small or double talk, and if I can't get what I need from you, I had no problem going over someone's head. I did that with one rep, and she got mad at me.

I told her, "Listen, we don't have to be friends and you don't have to like me. But you must respect me. I have a job to do. If you can't help me, I have to do what I have to do to get it done. Please know that it's nothing personal." We're very cool now.

More than anything, I've had to deal with being the only Black person. Often. My nickname for myself is The Lone Negro. I was the only Black person working on the *ABC ePrep* team—and the only woman in overnights at that point. I was the only Black person working on *The John Tesh Show*, and the only Black woman working at *Playboy Radio*.

There probably have been several people who've tried to sabotage me. Sadly, they don't understand that what God has for me is for ME. One incident I remember involved a woman I worked with at ABC. She and I were in the same place—just starting out and trying to make it. Since we were both working part-time, we had other jobs. She actually helped me get a part-time position at the office where she worked.

At that time, I was so tired that I was thinking about quitting *The Doug Banks* show. This chick actually went to my supervisor and said, "Miko is thinking of quitting. If she does, can I have her job?" My supervisor told me about it, and I was livid! Not only did I consider this chick my friend, but I had also helped her out when she got dental work because she didn't have family in the area. I could've killed her, but I played it cool. Because I wasn't the only one she tried screw over. She ended up dropping out of the business. Last I heard she was back in Cleveland working in the medical profession.

I've been blessed to have plenty of people who've taught me things—good and bad—and championed for me along the way. In no particular order...

LaJuana Johnson

LaDor Frank

Michelle Burden

DeDe McGuire

Willie Mae McIver

Denise Edwards
Ty Murrell
Sweet Willie Mitchell
Glenn Cosby
Steve Harris
Tom Joyner
Doug Banks
Neicy Tribbett
LaJoyce Brookshire

Trusting God and trusting my instincts—in that order have been in my survival toolbox. This business is very seductive, and it's easy to get caught up in it. If you have proper grounding where you understand the difference between right and wrong, you should be fine. And God loves me enough to keep me in spite of myself. I don't know that I've actually achieved my greatest accomplishment yet. I can say that I've worked consistently in national radio since 1995. I can say that I executive produced the 24-hour kickoff of *The Doug Banks Morning Show* on WBLS. But I believe that bigger and better things are in my future.

The industry is so different now than when I started. There are so many avenues to achieve radio stardom, and there's less respect for the actual craft of it than it used to be. Also, in so many instances, the people making decisions aren't familiar with exactly what it takes for us to do what we do. I tell young women to learn EVERYTHING. Being a personality is great, but if you work 10 years as a personality, you can't get a job announcing specials at the grocery store. Learn about the equipment, learn how to produce, learn how to write, learn what it takes to put a show together. Learn it all. Also, be nice to everyone. You never know who's doing what.

If you're a nice person, people will be more willing to help you or teach you. Also, be open to anything that's not illegal or immoral. I never planned to leave Texas. Now I've lived on both coasts. I never planned to work at Playboy Radio, but I learned so much about people, my faith, and myself. Also, I never planned to be a writer, yet writing has paid more than a few of my bills.

Miko Matthews with Kirk Franklin

SOCCERBIBL
I CALL THE SHOTS
WISH YOU WERE HERE
TOM DAVIES
THE MAN MACHINE

Mic Check 19

"Every Woman for Herself"

~by~

Sibrena Stowe-Geraldino

My first start in the music industry was around 1992-ish when I interned at Power 99 FM/ WUSL-FM in Philadelphia as a sound engineer, producer, and reporter in the Public Affairs Department. I started my company Stowe Communications, Inc., in September of 1996 and I provided full-service media and management to entertainers including publicity, media buys, and management.

Growing up, I was surrounded by people in the music and entertainment industry. I grew up in suburban Philly and the North East Bronx. One of my neighbors in the Bronx was Pumpkin - the first "producer," who was actually a Latino percussionist. His real name was Errol and he sort of introduced me to some of his friends in the business and they were all rappers. I was in love with any song from the Sugar Hill Gang.

My educational background is pretty diverse and perhaps different, so to speak. I was a student of music since elementary school and played the flute, piano, and keyboard until high school. I also was a broadcast major in North Penn High School under the direction of Mr. Earl Cardellino, and at Montgomery Community College.

I've always known that I wanted to be a journalist in the entertainment industry since fourth grade however, I didn't know about media buys and publicity until I was an adult. I think I was fully prepared for this since I could talk because I talked my ass off and asked a lot of questions for probably 2-year-olds! I fell in love with music when I was a baby, as my mother had all of the great albums from R&B, the Philly sound, and disco. I also studied acting, ballet, tap, and jazz at Freedom Theater in Philadelphia.

My greatest strength is identifying one's personality traits to hone in on that and making the world aware of that clients strengths/ traits and minimizing the clients weakness. I also am very talented at negotiating and placing an artist's brand on key television and radio spots...This is called a media buyer!

Some of the artists that I worked with include were A+, Chico DeBarge, Erykah Badu, Run DMC, NORE, Cash Money Millionaires, Juvenile, Lil Wayne, MJG & 8Ball, Solange, Beyonce's solo project "I AM Sasha Fierce", The Game, DJ Scratch, Petey Pablo, Czar Entertainment head Jimmy Rosemond, Brian McKnight, and others. I also managed rapper Foxy Brown when she was signed to Roc Nation and UGod from Wu-Tang Clan. And Kojo Bentil, Kedar Massenberg, Jacqueline "Jackie" Rhinehart, and Jean Riggins actually gave me my first start as a female entrepreneur in music.

I can tell a star by a certain "IT" factor. It's an undeniable thing that I can't quite sum up because it's several factors and either you have IT, or you don't!

For example, I had the opportunity to witness greatness with Beyonce and Destiny's Child. I met them when they were young, and I watched them grind harder than anyone. They went to every radio station, rehearsed, and experienced adversity, but they did not quit. By the time Beyonce was my media buying client, she was totally ready for her solo career and she soared. Also, DJ Scratch comes to mind when I look at who really had "IT." DJ Scratch worked harder as a DJ and producer than anyone I knew. He practiced and practiced and practiced! He walked like a star, talked like a star, and behaved like one. I find that those who have "IT" has been doing "it" since they were very young and wanted "it" or success, badly!

The most frustrating thing with artists is many of them are in this business for the glory. They may have some talent but to be successful it takes more than talent. I had incidents when Gorilla Black didn't want to do a press interview because the label set it up. He was upset because they forgot his per diem. That is self-sabotage. He didn't get the fact that the interview was to help his brand and promote his album. The label could care less if you act crazy because they'll put the album out with a minimum budget, recoup their money, and then hold up all of your future albums until they're either ready to release you, or if you're really someone they think can make a lot of money with, they'll string you along until they're ready to work with you, again!

Another moment was when I represented Spliff Starr, who was the hype man for Busta Rhymes. Spliff wasn't getting paid properly and complained to me about it. As his manager at the time, I suggested he not go on tour without a contract and a pay increase. He agreed and we met with Mona Scott about the terms. Things were going our way since Busta couldn't do a show without him—in our opinion. Two weeks went by and Spliff broke down and decided to go on tour without an increase. Needless to say, I couldn't work with anyone whom I thought wasn't willing to make smart decisions so that was the end of our relationship.

The most frustrating thing about my job was working with people who were not taking full advantage of their opportunities. A lot of clients were not business savvy and more interested in fame. You have to value the business aspect of your career just like rock n' roll artists and songwriters. I remember when I managed UGod from Wu-Tang, another guy who wasn't too savvy with business decisions. He'd go on tour and not know how much he would earn, at the end of the tour. I mean, there are numerous artists who make these mistakes and I honestly ask, where are they today?

Some of the challenges that I faced as a woman were more so with other women, at the height of Hip Hop. We didn't support one another the way we do now because, it was a boy's clique and we girls didn't want to band together, for whatever reason. The men stuck together and would only let in a few women in the inner circle. I was fortunate to be a part of a few label executives' inner circles and so at that time, it was every "woman" for herself.

Unfortunately, I wasn't able to make a lot of formidable relationships with other women unless I had to talk to them on a daily basis and that was maybe two handfuls of women. I mean let's keep it real, I was different, and my friends were mostly the label heads. I was professional and I never slept with the men. The men were my "brothers" and they respected me like a "sister."

I remember Kojo Bentil, who was the VP of Kedar Entertainment and Motown/Universal who was my friend and an attorney, saw me in jeans and he was shocked that I owned jeans. He laughed when he saw me and said, "Wow Sy, I never saw you dress down. You're always dressed to the tee." He was the first label head to give me business in 1996 and we've remained friends since. I ask him advice because I trust him completely.

I overcame challenges through growth and age. Now, I value my relationships with other women in the industry because we are truly kindred spirits. We've experienced so much at a young age, and we took a music genre to mainstream and internationally, so you have to respect that, protect our legacy, and share it with other women who aspire to do epic shit.

I enjoyed the perks of being a media buyer, publicist, and manager! I can't lie, I had the best tickets to any concert, boxing match, and award show. The perks and helping artists reach success are what I enjoyed the most!

My very first mentor is my mother who exposed me to music, theater, and writing. She encouraged me to explore my passions and to do it well. Next would be my TV Broadcasting instructor Mr. Earl Cardellino. I'm still in touch with him today! My other mentor, who helped me navigate through the media buying and advertising world is Sal Franco former partner of Gelwicks Advertising. Sal invested in me by buying my advertising clients in real estate (I placed real estate ads in the *New York Times* and *New York News Day*) and he also loaned me hundreds of thousands of dollars upfront to establish credit with the TV networks and radio networks.

Now, funny enough that my mentor is my husband Alex Geraldino. He has his MBA and so he's the one that asks me the hard questions like "What do I want to get out of representing a client" and "How can I maximize my talents for a client." Those are questions that I've never asked myself and now that my time is limited, I have to be sure I am going to have the time to give any potential client and to make sure it's mutually beneficial.

I have felt like quitting, and I did! I took a year off to figure out things when the industry turned digital. I can say I was afraid so, I moved into one of my houses in the Pennsylvania Pocono mountains and hibernated, prayed, and regrouped. This was the time that digital music took effect and budgets changed as well as the music industry changed. At some point, I got a call from a former Jimmy "Henchmen" Rosemond to handle his publicity during his criminal trial. I had to stay in Brooklyn near the courthouse for 2-3 months. Once the trial was over, I went back to the mountains, back to my small-town life.

A few weeks later, I got a call from the former security guard for Jimmy Rosemond, to talk to his friend named Maritza, who needed PR services. I met up with Maritza and a week later she introduced me to Alex Geraldino, now my husband.

One heart-singing moment was getting my client's cover and feature stories when I handled PR, and another was writing my first commercial and placing it during the BET Awards. I filmed that commercial at Roc the Mic, a recording studio owned at the time by Jay Z's partners Juan and Desiree Perez. They kindly gave me permission to use the facility, thanks to Danny "Moya" Reyes, then the studio manager. I hired an old friend who at the time worked at BET, Todd Tucker who is now married to Kandi Burress and is often seen on Real Housewives of Atlanta. Interestingly enough, my talent was the owner of the Diamond Shoe Laces, Caroline Egger, and former A & R exec, Micky Wright—who eventually married Lil Wayne's ex—Toya Wright. It's such a small world because Micky and Todd lived in NYC and became friends once Todd and Micky moved to Atlanta. I can say they met thanks to my project! I realized that this was the first time I did something for myself since one of my dreams was to write for TV.

I knew I was a bonafide behind the scenes rockstar when I was featured in *Black Enterprise* Magazine - the center spread and top feature story - while Master P and Puffy were on the cover. I was the only woman of color to own a media buying firm in the USA at the time, under 30, and a millionaire in the Hip Hop music industry. I guess my greatest accomplishment was when I was asked to be featured in a book called, "The New Color of Success".

I am proud of any artists who've sustained themselves, is still on top and doing things in the right way in terms of the music business. That's a rarity and so I definitely respect anyone who can last! Certainly, DJ Scratch, Beyonce, Lil Wayne, Cash Money and a few others are still relevant. My playlist is full of music from the height of Hip Hop. I love that era MOST so I'm listening to DMX, EVE, anything DJ Scratch & Swizz, Jay Z, Biggie, Cam'Ron and others.

I am truly insulted when ONLY Diddy, Jermaine Dupree, Jay Z and Dame Dash, and other men in the industry get to tell their stories. It's definitely not fair because, behind each of these guys, there is a Suzanne DePasse. I know our stories are compelling, especially when you have moms like me who had to sacrifice and work long hours for our clients.

I would tell my younger self to be a part of a clique because they'll stick together, usually, and continue to do business together. I would also tell my younger self to have more patience with people because you never know their full story. I've learned many lessons in the music business, that I apply today. The most important thing is to believe in yourself and know that mistakes are ok because you now know what not to do.

I always tell women in the business these two things, know the brand, and don't eat where you shit. This means, don't sleep with anyone that you work for so that they'll respect you and know your brand or artist. Being respected is important, so you can be heard. I never wore jeans to a meeting, folks only saw me in a business suit and heels, and I've never slept with anyone to get ahead!

My deepest regret is that I didn't take my friend Anton Marchands' advice, to write music. Anton was an A&R manager under Steve Stoute and for Tone & Poke. Anton is Foxy Brown's eldest brother. One day he asked, "You write, right? Well, why don't you write music?" Can you believe I told him I don't have time for that because I'm a "real writer"? #SMH

I miss the late 90s and early 2000s in Hip Hop because we were the pulse of the music industry. We made many platinum hits; we went hard on the streets and radio, and we were young and fearless! I miss the record release parties too!

If given the opportunity, I would definitely do more media buys. I don't foresee myself handling publicity unless it was an amazing project. I'd prefer to help brand music executives, instead of an artist. Execs get it and they make shit happen.

I'd like to think that I keep my pinky toe in the music business because it's something that I know, love, and I do well. Currently,

I'm doing a few things with Ruff Ryders partner Chivon Dean. For the most part, I'm focused on my soccer team New Jersey Teamsterz FC and that's similar yet, different. I'm having a lot of fun learning about soccer.

I am currently the CEO of New Jersey Teamsterz Football Club, a men's professional and developmental soccer club based in Bayonne, New Jersey. My husband Alexsi Geraldino and I founded the club in 2017 and our journey from semi-pro to pro soccer is streaming on the Discovery Channel reality series called, "I Quit". The series documented myself and other entrepreneurs leaving something - for me - it was the Hip Hop industry, for soccer. I fell in love with the overall sport of soccer as well as, the business structure and stadium operations. I also found a way to integrate Hip Hop with soccer, so let's say, I am back behind the mic!

I am also a content editor at *DREW* Magazine, a quarterly lifestyle magazine by Drew Barrymore. I love working the Drew and our small team of talent, mostly women, in media and publishing. I fact-check and proofread each issue and make suggestions or not before we go to print. You can call me the truth-seeker, LOL. In all seriousness, I manifested this job. I watched DREW's show and was so inspired by her enthusiasm that I googled her team and found out she had just launched a magazine. I followed her creative team on Instagram and that same day, a post for a fact-checker popped up. Obviously, I applied and was persistent and here I am, almost two years in and I'm not only on the masthead but I get to work with some iconic women in media.

In 2020, during the pandemic, I became the first Black female principal owner of a professional club in U.S. history and the City of Bayonne and Hudson County awarded me a proclamation during International Women's Month. Soccer was relatively new for me so I had learning curves, and challenges to overcome and I am grateful for those experiences because I've grown tremendously. I am also a content editor at *DREW* Magazine, a quarterly lifestyle magazine by Drew Barrymore. There are a lot of "I's" here, but it took a Village to get me to this level and a team of people helped me realize my dreams. I am forever enriched, and I appreciate every person who helped make me a better businesswoman. Transitioning into soccer has been one of the best highlights of my life so far, and I'm just getting started!

Sibrena Stowe-Geraldino and Swizz Beatz

Mic Check 20

"Grace Under Pressure"

~by~

Mary Moore

I have primarily been a publicist; however, I began rather differently and took some interesting career paths. In a nutshell, though, a couple highlights are that I was in Publicity at RCA Records (8 years), and at Arista Records (2 years). However, I functioned as a concert director at Radio City Music Hall (6 years), a Talent Scout for *Star Search* (1 season), personal assistant to Gilda Radner of "Saturday Night Live," (2 years) and began it all in the U.S. Navy, as an Information Specialist/Broadcast Journalist.

I always belonged to the glee club or chorale in school and played the guitar whenever the occasion called for it. My military training (Dept. of Defense Information School) definitely prepared me not only for the record industry, but also for life. The military way of having more than one plan in mind, in case the first one doesn't pan out, has served me well.

hoto: Mary More with Luenell

After the military, I re-entered civilian life at home in New York, and sought a job. I wanted to get into radio, one of the areas that I had worked in the military (Armed Forces Radio & Television Service), but that didn't work out. So, I worked various temp jobs, in order to make a living and get my feet wet in the civilian work world, which usually turned into job offers. The primary temp job that launched me into the entertainment industry was that of working at NBC-TV in New York; while working there in Human Resources, I was hired as personal assistant to comedian Gilda Radner at *Saturday Night Live* after her first Emmy win. After that, the rest of my career path occurred primarily via networking.

My greatest strength is the gift of gab, affinity for the English language, creativity, and ability to multi-task effectively. Also, strict parents kept me together and Catholic school (grammar & high school) made me focused. My sense of humor has also definitely helped.

The minute I first heard music as a child, I was in love! It transported me to faraway places, which was great for a daydreaming kid like me. And different types of music intrigued me—I had, and still have, favorites in most genres, even in country, classical, show tunes, folk, salsa, pop, rock, and other music.

Music was always a part of my life! I sang, danced (tap and ballet lessons) and played guitar. My parents kept music playing at home, and had eclectic tastes themselves, so I was treated to a variety of sounds while growing up. I occasionally auditioned for Broadway and off-Broadway shows, and competed in two beauty contests, usually doing well in the talent part. I joined a girl group named The Magic Touch, after returning from the Navy. The group's big hit was "Step Into My World." I'm comfortable in the spotlight, but I prefer behind the scenes much more.

To be honest, I was more of an R&B kid, and came to Hip Hop late, after working in the industry and being exposed to more of it. I gravitated toward Hip Hop songs like Pharcyde's "Passing Me By" and Camp Lo's "Luchini." I also dug Apache's "Gangsta Bitch," and early tunes by Queen Latifah ("U.N.I.T.Y") and LL Cool J ("Around The Way Girl"). Later, I got into Brand Nubian, Jay Z, and Bone, Thugs & Harmony. I think my favorite may have been by a Hip Hop group that I worked with at RCA Records - "Hell Bound," by The Almighty RSO. The first R&B song I fell in love with is really hard to say. I've always loved 70s vocal group songs, like from The Stylistics, The Chi-Lites, The Dramatics, Blue Magic, and solo artists like Otis Redding, with "Try A Little Tenderness," a song that builds so beautifully, starting with a slow tempo and ending up at a frenzied pace. My all-time favorite jam? I can't choose just one—that's like asking a mother which child she loves more!

I have been blessed to have worked with a long list of artists. However, some highlights...at RCA, I worked with Tyrese, SWV, the Wu-Tang Clan, Mobb Deep; at Arista, I worked with Whitney Houston, Jennifer Holliday, Dionne Warwick, Jermaine Jackson, The Braxtons, Milli Vanilli, and along the way at various times, I worked with Gloria Gaynor, Heather Headley, Freddie Jackson and many, many other superstar talents.

Usually, when all the pieces fell into place, and multiple areas and teams worked together, projects humming like a well-oiled machine. The reinforcement of firing on all cylinders usually produced great results. When everything clicked, it was magical, and the superstars were able to do their best work.

My favorite project was that of RCA Records singer/songwriter Cherokee. Cherokee was a publicist's dream—she had a multi-layered story, with something of interest for various types of media folks. She was also very easy to work with. She was not only beautiful, but she was also very talented as well. One of my Cherokee project highlights was getting her on the cover of *Time Out New York* magazine (which was accompanied by huge NYC bus shelters with her face on them), along with a fashion spread in *Essence* magazine, a feature in *Vibe* magazine, and all sorts of television shows. All that visibility even garnered her some modeling opportunities.

With all of these opportunities being made available, I was frustrated that all the pieces didn't come together. The public was seeing Cherokee's face and name in a big way, but not hearing her music at the same level, in order to connect the dots. It was one of the things which really frustrated me, because sometimes I was far more passionate about some acts than the label was since I personally liked their music and/or liked them as people. But there was definitely a "priority system" in place, sometimes unbeknownst to me. One of the moments that make me smile is being thanked on BET live, by Cherokee. That seldom happened, that an artist thanked their publicist by name. I was so taken by her graciousness.

Personally, I don't think that being a woman in the industry was very challenging. (I think that being African American was more of a challenge than being female.) Maybe I view this differently because of my military background. I had a goal of mastering any room. I just studied what the dynamic of the room was and sat back until I could ascertain a specific role there for myself.

I enjoyed being "first" in some of my positions. I especially loved giving my parents more and more reasons to be proud of me. They kept every clipping I appeared in, in a scrapbook. When

I rose to being the highest-ranking female executive (Director level) at Radio City Music Hall and appeared in *Ebony* and *JET* magazines, I was definitely pleased—doing the best job possible has always been my mantra and is probably what propelled me into being a workaholic. Subsequently, rising to Vice President at RCA Records wasn't a first, but for me, it was a personal triumph to reach that level, an affirmation that hard work pays off.

When I was met with resistance on a project by someone who did not like my ideas, I'd gather some allies who agreed with my point of view. So, when it wasn't just my idea or agenda, it would sometimes be received better. Or plant the seed with someone else who they'd be more receptive to, so that they could run with the ball, and get my objective accomplished that way.

I've encountered all sorts of females in the industry and have found that jealousy and insecurity usually fuel sabotage. I had a nemesis when I worked for Gilda Radner and our dislike for each other was mutual, so I usually just tried to ignore her, even though it was easy for her to get under my skin. Also, "know-it-all" women also drive me nuts—I've run into a few of them along the way. No one knows it all! I was able to diffuse one of them by just calling her bluff on a conference call (which was embarrassing for her) and with another, I always made it a point to highlight her shortcomings/weaknesses to others (fight fire with fire), every time she attempted to berate the quality of my work.

I had a few special folks who guided were my champions and welcomed me into the fray—first, veteran entertainment executive Scott Sanders, who hired me at Radio City Music Hall; then, Melani Rogers at Arista Records, who gave me my first label job; and the late Skip Miller, who recruited me over to RCA Records. And I learned quite a bit by watching veteran PR maven Terrie Williams, during my time at her firm.

When faced with challenges, I didn't necessarily share that with anyone in the industry; I often called and spoke with my parents, who were down-to-earth and logical, and usually able to calm and ground me to the point that I could make sound decisions. Turning to people that you trust, who are outside of the industry, can afford you a fresh perspective. And yes, at times I considered quitting, but I didn't. Mostly for financial reasons! That is REAL TALK! On a personal note, I regret not purchasing my apartment on the Upper West Side of Manhattan when I had the chance, and the funds.

Honestly, I miss the money, big label budgets, and the perks. I also miss the in-person sharing of ideas with a team (marketing meetings were sometimes quite interactive and fun). And I miss getting invited to events. I also miss how the industry *used to be*, prior to the internet era. But time marches on, and we have to evolve with it.

Ultimately, I was bursting with pride when I finally broke the glass ceiling at RCA Records and was made a Vice President. For other moments, I'm very proud of the accomplishments of those who were my interns at various times, and seeing those Platinum and Gold record plaques on my apartment walls still gives me a sense of pride.

Some of the aspects for a while there, I really enjoyed the travel. Going to Washington, DC for BET's *Teen Summit* on Saturdays, or to Los Angeles for *Soul Train* tapings or award shows—that was fun. It gave me my lasting love for fine hotels.

My most embarrassing moment had to be when I picked up Arista Records duo Milli Vanilli at Kennedy Airport in New York City, when they first came to the United States, and I took them to lunch. They opted not to speak English at all, so I sat at the table feeling very out of place, as they communicated with each other only in German. Other diners sitting around us felt sorry for me.

I think that I really realized my value when I began to be included on non-Urban music projects, particularly at RCA. Being consulted on the Urban market value of Pop artists, and working on those projects (like Christina Aguilera, the Dave Matthews Band, Robyn) was very self-affirming.

I'm proud of any artist that I've assisted in their career journey, in any way! I have a real sense of nostalgia when I hear old songs that I worked, being played on the radio now. I think back to those times, and the success that accompanied the song and the artist. I love having those great memories.

All I have to say about women being left out of stories being told is…That's show biz! Poetic license is usually taken, with most stories. And it will vary, depending on who is telling the story. Those behind the mic are usually the unsung heroes. I like to liken myself to a puppeteer, in the background, pulling strings to make things happen. Folks don't need to see me—they see my work. That's my satisfaction and I would tell my younger self to slow down and savor those moments. Don't forget to have fun!

To young women aspiring to work in this industry I say: Always have a back-up plan. Never assume that anything is permanent. Get as many skills under your belt as possible. Always network—your personality/people skills are often your best calling card. And, if it becomes necessary to re-brand or re-invent yourself, don't hesitate to do it. And—two things to aim for—residual income (things that continue to pay you in the future) and multiple streams of income (self-explanatory).

There will always be a sticky situation one may encounter, I advise to stay calm, consider all sides of the issue, and not make any hasty decisions. Like the deodorant tag line...Never let 'em see you sweat. Work on exhibiting Grace Under Pressure. Women are expected to be emotional, so avoid that in this business. (Scream and holler when you get home...)

RCA Records closed down their Black Music Division in 2001, two weeks after 9/11. I didn't receive a percentage of the company; however, the 401K plan and profit sharing were very valuable. Having an employment contract negotiated by an entertainment attorney was key for me at RCA Records, especially when the Black Music Division was dissolved. I continued on, though, hanging out my own shingle and RCA was my first client as an independent publicist. And, moving forward, I didn't limit myself to only music projects. Diversification was key.

From the music business I learned to not take too many things personally. And, to show respect to all levels of the industry—today's mailroom guy may be the president of the company in a few years. Lots of other behind-the-scenes folks have been very valuable in assisting me along the way—they are often the important, trusted gatekeepers for the moguls.

The most important survival skill, for me, is a sense of humor. Gotta laugh some things off, and not take them too seriously. The entertainment business is not saving lives or creating cures for diseases—it's show business. A balanced sense of humor makes you more resilient.

Today, I'm an independent publicist, still working hard, and making a living! The industry has changed quite a bit, like with the advent of the internet, but I just keep rocking and rolling right along with it. And being an independent publicist comes with a freedom that a label job did not—I can use my varied resources/ relationships on projects, regardless of what "department" they might be considered, without stepping on anyone else's toes. I can also pick and choose the projects I want to work on, from those that are offered to me, not like at a label, where you must work on what they assign you to, whether you like it or not.

Anyway, at the end of the day - It's just show biz.

Our dear, sweet Mary Moore submitted her story shortly before she departed this life on April 5, 2019. We love and miss her dearly. We know Mary is in heaven shining brightly wearing her 'color of the day.'

Mary Moore with SWV

Mic Check 21

"Slay Those Demons"

~by~

Lonai Mosley

My earliest memories of falling in love with music go as far back as the 1960s, to the tender age of two or three growing up in New Haven, Connecticut. My Dad, Nate Mosley, was a founding member and vocal tenor of "Rock-and-Roll Hall of Fame inductees, The Five Satins, known for their classic hit "In the Still of the Night." Dad would lift me up onto his six foot four shoulders and seemingly glide us into the dopamine filled world of recording, rehearsal studios, and live stage show performances.

Oh! How I loved witnessing the soothing Doo-wop sounds of their velvety harmonies, and the magical way the accompanying musician's fingers would effortlessly cascade over string instruments and piano keys. The effect it had on the audience was not only a site to behold, but one I felt an immediate connection with. I was entranced each time I experienced it.

Our home was filled with all genres of music from Mozart to Motown and beyond. Daddy was my multifaceted superhero, and the band members, who had become my uncles, would praise and reward me with compliments for being cute and quiet with candy for a job well done during those long-lasting sessions. Behaving well wasn't a challenge for me, because I understood, even as a toddler and adolescent, that during this period some of the most turbulent times in Black history were happening. The struggle of the Civil Rights movement I saw living in a city where the dichotomy of Yale University met the Black Panther party headquarters, presented a fixed reality in our city. I knew that entering the musical "Zone" was an invigorating, safe space, in which creativity could blossom and provide open access to all the "Good Things" life had to offer. It was where I felt accepted for just being me, encouraged with a warm welcome-home style embrace. And the place I wanted to thrive in and reside forever.

I was always a natural visual and musically inclined artist, who from an early age was filled with curiosity about the world around me. Growing up in an artistic environment had its advantages. My Mom created all types of art, drawing, painting, and crafting, and my dad's musical background exposed me to the possibilities of pursuing the Arts professionally. I listened to my favorite go-to selections on my own record player, singing along, reading every label liner note from the inside out of the album flat, because I was so curious about the music production process. I wanted to know who wrote the lyrics, played, and sang on those all-time favorite cuts. Music motivated me to draw, write plays, and direct mini musicals where I charged my participating friend's parents 50 cents to see their children perform live renditions of the songs in the shows I directed.

An eclectic mix of artists and musical genres was the norm in our home. My Dad being a Doo-Wop vocalist, self-taught jazz flutist, guitarist, writer, and enthusiast listened to and played with some of the greats like Lionel Hampton, The Righteous Brothers, Miles, Thelonious Monk, Dizzy, Coltrane, Sarah Vaughn, Ella Fitzgerald, Billie Holiday, and others. My Mom introduced me to other locally grown Doo-Wop groups, 1950s "Oldies but Goodies," and Classic Rock of the 60s, like Janice Joplin, Hendricks, Santana, The Beatles, Dionne Warwick, Soul, and R&B. Each of these musical experiences deepened my exposure and appreciation for a vast array of musical styles and tastes. I consider the Blaxploitation film era and 70s Funk, Disco, Aretha Franklin, Motown's Supremes, Smokey Robinson, and The Jackson Five - who performed an unforgettable concert at Yale Bowl in New Haven in the early 70s—to have left indelible memories on my impressionable soul.

Early rap-poetry moved me and continues to be some of my favorites. Gil Scott Heron, The Last Poets, and Reggae music, which I adore to this day. The first commercial Hip Hop songs I remember listening to were introduced to me by my cousins who were huge fans of the Sugar Hill Gang's "Rapper's Delight," Apache, Run DMC's "Run DMC" and "King of Rap". When DJ and radio mixtapes made their way to Connecticut from The Bronx, Queensbridge, and South Jamaica queens,, it was on! Public Enemy, LL Cool J, Kool Herc, the radio station WBLS' *Mr. Magic* show were it. "Funk You Up" by Angie Stone's group, The Sequence, Africa Bambaataa, Grandmaster Flash, Fab 5 Freddie, Busy Bee, Curtis Blow's "The Breaks," Kool Moe Dee and The Treacherous Three, to name a few, and even Blondie quickly became familiar staples on the scene.

After accelerating through West Haven High school in three years, I enrolled in college at age 16 and a half, choosing to major in Mass Communications and TV Production with a minor in Theater at Southern Connecticut State University. Simultaneously, I moved out of my mom's house to live with my 24-year-old "Boyfriend." My side hustles would continue. AM classes, 1PM- Front desk receptionist at CT Savings Bank, and 5-8:30pm, evening classes. Hair braiding and make-up clients got in where they fit in. When an opportunity for work presented itself, I left New Haven and junior year in my rear view and relocated to NYC to pursue the Arts professionally. Resuming my college education would return later in the 90s after a dry spell briefly happened and I was collecting unemployment.

An NYC Department of Labor employee told me they would pay for the career training of my choice at any vocational school or college. I said, "Any school?" And the answer was yes, any school. That fall semester I enrolled in the first of two years of classes for entertainment marketing, entertainment Law, and film production at NYU School of Continuing Studies Certificate Program where I fine-tuned additional skills in contractual management, deal negotiation and film making skills. Twelve years into the School of Hard Knocks had been my education until that point. No level of college education could have prepared me for the tough as nails, and at times brutal corporate world of the entertainment industry. It was where each fortune 500 major record label I worked with had its own corporate culture, and the higher profile its artist roster was, and more dollars were at stake, the more cutthroat the environment could be.

When I relocated from New Haven to Harlem in the early 80's, I saw some of the MCs I loved perform live, even finding my way to appearing in several of their music videos. Carefully crafted cardboard boxes were broken down and leveled out to create platforms on city sidewalks for break dancers wearing shell top Adidas, Lee jeans, Kangol hats and Gazelle glasses, While Ggraffiti tagged "Red Bird" subway trains set the backdrop and tone for the gritty urban landscape during those times, and the deal was sealed. I was staying.

I've been fortunate to have had numerous up close and personal opportunities to observe, learn from, being mentored by and working with some of the best and most powerful industry leaders and artists known to date. I have witnessed new labels emerge and established ones, fold. Survived mergers, acquisitions, and hostile takeovers. Been the right hand to several levels of executives and artists, performing varied tasks as we launched and sustained careers, and soothed the wings of those who crashed and burned in a multitude of positions - both from the inside and out - of major and independent record labels. Throughout these experiences, I discovered my natural gifts, talents, and abilities, each driven by my passion for international marketing, event and video production and gaining insight to those industry mechanics I had longed to know. However, it all came with a price. Sacrifice filled long hours, seeing way more than any eye should, minimal compensation for my efforts. And placing Motherhood on hold. I was developing into a bonafide demon slayer who bore the stripe-covered scars I earned.

During the early morning hours in the summer of 1988, while out and about on the bustling streets of Manhattan, I remember thinking, "Where is everyone who's anyone?" Fueled by my mission to "Break into the business and learn" the mechanics of the corporate side of the entertainment industry, was an envisioned pathway to access and diversion from the struggle of my solo artistic journey. I'd often hit the pavement before the sticky humidity of NYC ruined my polished and professional interview outfit, make-up, and quaffed hair. As a routine, I would pick up copies of the

New York Times, *Variety*, *Backstage* and free *Village Voice* newspapers to scour the classified ads for entertainment industry auditions and employment opportunities.

One morning, I made a beeline from the suffocating morning crush of the subway to my makeshift office located in the cool and comfortable, centrally located 8th floor lobby of the Marriott Marquis Hotel lounge. Overlooking Times Square, from the massive window, I felt especially energized while munching on my favorite Zabar's bakery spinach croissant and sipping a cup of lemon tea with honey. Something clicked as my eyes locked in on a tiny listing in the *Village Voice* for a receptionist position at a record label. Confident I was a quick learner, and an articulate communicator, I knew I could easily answer front desk phones and dropped one of the handful of dimes I had into the payphone's coin slot. I dialed the number from the listing and expressed interest in scheduling an interview. The voice on the other end asked me if I could come in today. Little did I know, I was speaking directly with the CEO, who was always the first one in and the last to leave the East Village office. He developed a habit of answering the office phones before his staff arrived and was obviously in urgent need of a receptionist. The interview consisted of "What do you know about the music industry?"

Although my answer may have been shallow, it was enough for him to respond, "You don't know much, when can you start?" The label was Profile Records who had signed RUN DMC, Dana Dane, Dr Jekyll and Mr. Hyde, Rob Base, Judy Torres, Allyson Williams, and several other artists who were on the fast track to Hip Hop and R&B stardom. I knew right then and there that the early bird does get the worm. My greatest strengths were an innate drive to succeed, being a quick study, creative vision, personable demeanor, an ear for music, eye for visuals, strong communications skill, adaptability to a variety of environments, and an easy on the eye physical appearance.

Before I worked at record labels, I was an aspiring make-up artist for the Broadway show Black and Blue, starring legendary Atlantic Records LaVerne Baker who took me under her wing and on the road with Ruth Brown and Etta James. Song writing with my own 4-track home-based recording studio, performing minor gigs at CBGB's and Danceteria, a Madonna haunt. And steady work as a bartender at the live music hot spot, The Cellar Restaurant on the Upper west side. Home to regulars like Patti Labelle, who would sit and order her chicken gizzards, recording session musicians, singers, and then unsigned Johnny Kemp and Me'lisa Morgan. I witnessed and anticipated whose limo would pull up and sweep who away from the house band next.

Music video extra work came calling one day while in the Village with friends, when Big Daddy Kane's people approached. Then Oran "Juice" Jones, Lolita Holloway, Kool Mo Dee, and others. I turned down a $250 a week assistant offer from the in-demand music video production company, owned by Lionel Martin, as I frequented the Apollo Theatre, which led to an invitation to work as a make-up apprentice on the pilot season of *Showtime at the Apollo*. My family was so excited when they saw my name in the credit scroll.

Ralph Cooper, Sr., Master of Ceremonies, and creator of Amateur Night at The Apollo then invited me to become his personal assistant. Assisting Mr. Cooper with his make-up, hair, dressing and handling admin tasks until his death from cancer in 1992, was such an inspiration to me. He was the first African American man to secure a major studio production deal with

Paramount Pictures, where he produced feature films as far back as the 1930s. He was a choreographer for Shirley Temple's *Poor Little Rich Girl*, a radio personality who created and hosted the "Amateur Hour show" in the 1930s. He was also a successful screenwriter, and actor, Hollywood had nick-named "Dark Gable." In one of his films titled *Dark Manhattan*, he played a Racketeer determined to rule the Harlem numbers scene. He also had starred with then newcomer, the legendary Lena Horne, after whom he called me "Little Lena," because he said I reminded him of her. He encouraged me to know, "You can successfully do more than one thing well," and his original creations would become the format for *American Idol, X Factor, The Voice* and many of the Talent shows known today.

Atlantic International Marketing, Warner Brothers, Elektra, Universal Music Group, PolyGram, Motown, and other labels would become the university in which I would learn and develop as I devoured the information I was exposed to and needed to master.

While honing my skill sets, I acquired an in-depth understanding of the business of music. Publishing, A&R, marketing, branding, promotion, publicity, and much more allowed me to learn to negotiate, and broker my own firsts. A six-figure deal as a rep for an emerging music video director with SONY 550 music, then segueing into a video producer/director myself was the springboard for indie film and television production, where writing, voice over acting and coordinating producer duties for Spike TV in the Paramount family was all like a dream gift wrapped-up in a not so neatly tied bow.

My initial five-year plan from the late 1980s to "Break into and learn" the mechanics of the corporate side of the entertainment industry morphed into twenty-five plus, years of consecutive work, holding down various positions, titles and leveling up through the ranks, in numerous departments and companies.

The pinnacle and end of my executive music career pivoted in 1998 with what began as a horrible day, after being fired from my job at Columbia Jazz on a mere "technicality." Due to the culmination of a tumultuous couple of months at the externally pristine 35th floor Madison Avenue location we called 550. With my eyes set on an available Product Manager's position, I was diligent about mastering the creation of all the marketing collateral I knew I could design with the given opportunity. I produced posters, palm cards, and promotional Tchotchkes. I loved being able to use all my creative skill sets. The department head VP traveled abroad frequently, leaving me to handle project coordinator responsibilities, administrative work, and more in his absence. It was right up my alley to be self-sufficient, and I did my best to rise to the occasion. Embracing the freedom to create and the safe space to create in was critical.

I had pressed through a series of eye opening and misogynistic experiences over the years, and recently through walking in on a different department VP in the midst of receiving fellatio when I needed paperwork signed. Instead of him being embarrassed, I received a sinister grin when I waved the document for signature. "OK, see me when you can," I said while backing out of the unlocked office door. So, when my current VP mentioned one of the Senior VP's had noticed my work and that a lunch meeting was being set up with him, what should have been a moment of excitement for me, under "normal" circumstances, triggered an immediate sense of dread. It was no secret that Quid-Pro-Quo was running rampant in the artist on executive and executive on support staff realm. I had seen first-hand the reality of the corporate culture throughout various labels, and under no uncertain terms, I knew what "Alone" time meant with Senior executives there. I declined, saying I wouldn't accept the meeting or any position where I would have to compromise myself for a fifty-thousand-dollar a year job.

The protocol for getting paid during this pre-digital scanning era was that my supervisor instructed me to physically sign his name on my weekly timesheets and initial them accordingly before submitting them to HR for payment processing. This particular morning, I received a call from HR asking me if I had signed my timesheets. I said, yes, I always do as my supervisor was in London, and had instructed me to do so. The HR rep said he spoke to the VP who had denied that directive, accusing me of fraud and dismissed me immediately. Check Mate.

I was devastated, alone and without anyone to come to my defense. I saw no recourse but to pack up my belongings as I looked around one last time at all the contributions I made while employed there now posted on the walls and stacked on my desk. I grabbed a couple of promotional mementos and headed towards the elevator. I was about to exit the lobby when I saw a familiar face in passing. I said, "Good morning." He stopped and said, "I remember you from Motown."

I was happy he remembered, "Yes, I was Andre Harrel's number three assistant when he first moved over from Uptown Records to become President."

He asked, "What are you doing now?"

Screaming in my head was, *I love the music but should have remained a fan*. Maintaining my composure, I responded, "Actually today happens to be my last day working here, and I'm not sure what I'll be doing next."

"Why don't you come by my office on Monday, I may have something for you." he offered.

The meeting on 57th Street and 7th Avenue was scheduled for 11am. I arrived at 10:45 and waited anxiously in the reception area. After a few minutes a female executive invited me into a corner office with a view of the city. I curiously sat down for the interview, as I had no indication what the opportunity held. After exchanging light pleasantries, the interviewer handed me a piece of paper which unbeknown to me would later evolve into a marketing plan I would be charged with adapting. He gave me a few minutes to review and respond to the scenarios in question on what undoubtedly was an aptitude assessment. My excitement grew as it became apparent that the responsibilities described in the document aligned with my previous experience, areas of interest, and some. I confidently completed the challenge in a few minutes and handed it back to him.

He reviewed it, said "Good." and offered me the position on the spot. I was to become the National Advertising strategist for the startup company in the process of launching shortly. Several names on the company's client roster and those they provided legal representation for consisted of Chaka Khan, Larry Graham, WNBA player Lisa Leslie, actress Lynn Whitfield, and many others. Last, and certainly not least on the list was the legendary artist himself, formally known as Prince. He and his attorney's firm, L. Londel McMillian, PC had formed an alliance and I was officially invited to be a part of the marketing, advertising, and distribution team for this latest venture which was on the forefront of the independent internet music distribution machine called the NorthStar Distribution Company. I stayed with them for three years.

Given the opportunity, I did build trust with various artists I worked with. At times suggesting flattering clothing, hairstyles, nutritional supplements, venue set up, fielding radio, press and sales. Song structures, and choices, house, or pet sitting, and just being a soundboard with insightful advice or moral support. Some of the artists I've worked with were super sensitive, or their ego so massive that they were their own worst enemies. It's challenging and heartbreaking to watch someone so talented unnecessarily self-destruct, or self-sabotage their own careers because of uncontrollable human traits or toxic addictions.

The most frustrating thing about my job responsibilities at times was not being able to complete assignments due to some form of a toxic or threatening occurrence. Like being exposed to backbiting behavior from co-workers, drug induced bad behaviors from cohorts or artists I had to manage, unwanted sexual advances from men in positions of authority, not enough financial compensation, or no corporate support for projects I considered to have so much potential.

Some gender challenges I faced as a woman working in the music industry included attempts at being pressured to perform sexual acts to maintain employment by men in positions of authority. Quid Pro Quo. Physically fighting off being overpowered if left alone with the wrong person because of my petite stature, taken advantage of for my kind demeanor, not being taken seriously or dismissed for my professional input while working with misogynistic males, and last but certainly not least being undercompensated for the amount of work and successes I achieved, to name a few.

Before the "Me Too" movement, I realized that some bad behaviors were rampant throughout the industry and considered to be an unwritten rule and part of the process. So, I often changed gears to avoid confrontation, stood my ground, sought new opportunities, ignored the advances if possible, or quit, believing better opportunities would surface. And they usually did.

I've been blessed with several mentors over the years, and one of my favorites was Senior TV producer, Lilian Smith. As the first African American woman to successfully produce and sustain a 20 year career as an Emmy award winning daytime TV talk show producer since the late 1960s, she was a force to be reckoned with. Small in stature, yet mighty in power, as a media icon, Lillian handled the industry, men, and Phil Donahue in a way in which no one else could have at a time when women, and especially women of color didn't have the opportunity to do so. She was a real-life fearless pioneer, if ever there was one, who shared her knowledge, wisdom, and feedback in a direct and nurturing manner.

These days seeing videos, documentaries, or hearing music from artists I've worked with is at times surreal. Especially ones from the 90s, where the opportunities to secure work were seamless, and the financial compensation could be vast. I think, *Wow! I did contribute to that success.* I'm happy they sustained and survived. I was really there until it didn't make sense for me to be there anymore. Until it was time to pivot towards my own successes, no longer focused on making millionaires more millions. with minimal recognition or compensation. I wanted a family of my own before it was too late, and an age-appropriate lifestyle I could manage.

It is most definitely time for WBTM to receive not only equal pay, but equal recognition for the detail oriented, nurturing and insightful impact that comes with successes created as a result of that Black Girl Magic.

Advice I always give to young students, aspiring artists, entertainers, and future industry executives is that we only get to do 365 x 80ish, so be proactive with your time, it's valuable and temporary. Every experience is either a lesson or a teaching moment. Live your life with intention. Dream specific. Know your why, it's your own purpose. Overstand your assignment. Hard work does result in reward and can surpass talent. Focus on developing your gifts, talents, and abilities, because they translate to dollars, otherwise you wouldn't have been born with them. Be kind, relationships are everything, and it does take a Village. Be helpful, Karma is reciprocal. Above all else, create energy, manifest dreams, and be grateful for something each day because thoughts and words do have power. Today, all my life and industry experiences have evolved into an incredible journey fueled by faith, wisdom, and the ability to navigate this crazy, temporal plane we call Earth. I believe we are all spirits having a human experience for a while until our purpose here is done. I can honestly say that throughout all the hardships, challenges, heartbreaks, near death experiences, and more, I've survived for a reason. I feel blessed to be able to translate the lessons and stripes I've earned into many revenue streams. Compensation appears in my life in miraculous ways. I still get paid to create art, and for that I'm so grateful. Am an Arts in Education Advocate who answered the call to teach skills so that the next in line can win. I am able to Executive Produce various projects, upcycle, and sell my visual art. I get to enjoy travel, the ocean, snorkeling, and am a Level One Diver working toward obtaining Open Water Certification, and I am a mom to an amazing 21-year-old son.

And… I'm pleased to be walking and working with Angels.

Lonai Mosley with Artist Maliwayz

Mic Check 22

"Make Key Decisions"

~by~

Gwendolyn Quinn

Growing up in the DMV, known as Washington, DC, Maryland, and Virginia, I'm not completely surprised that my journey eventually led to a career in the music and record industries.

My love for music, especially Black Music, was undeniable. I grew up listening to music in my family's home, curated by my parents and my older brother on the 45rpm and the 10-inch LP vinyl on the record player. As I grew older, I listened to music on Howard University's WHUR-FM and its "Quiet Storm" format with the late radio personality Melvin Lindsey. The "Quiet Storm" format was created by entrepreneur and media mogul Cathy Hughes. My favorite pastime growing up was attending concerts at the historic Constitution Hall, Warner Theatre, the Lowe's Palace Theater, along with the outdoor venue, the Carter Barron Amphitheater, and summer concerts on the National Mall, and the Capital Centre arena in Landover, Maryland, among many other venues and clubs in the DMV. All the popular music artists came through Chocolate City, and I saw almost everyone that came to town.

While I was in my senior year of high school, I had started creating a substantial following of Black women in the DMV, who was part of the hair braiding movement, which had a major resurgence in Black America in the late seventies and early eighties. During the early days of that movement, I worked as a braider at the Miya Gallery, founded by the late Vernard Gray, the beloved Washington, DC activist, and impresario. Amid the Black Arts Movement, the Miya Gallery, then located on 11th Street, N.W., was a place of creative expression, which was one of the first African braiding shops in the country and on the east coast. The gallery was also the home to visual artists, photographic exhibits, and poets who regularly performed their latest works. The late music journalist and musician Greg Tate, then a student at Howard University would perform his works at the Miya Gallery celebrating African American musicians.

Before moving to New York and still in high school, I would visit my cousins in Brooklyn during the summers and I was fascinated by the music and culture scene there. I had also discovered Frankie Crocker and WBLS radio station and thought that was the best station I have ever heard, next to WHUR-FM, of course. The vibrance of New York City was infectious. It was at that time that I decided that I would move to New York after I finished high school.

In March 1980, and 18 years old, with two suitcases and three hundred dollars to my name, I boarded a Greyhound bus to move to the Empire State. I moved in with my two cousins who resided in the Crown Heights section of Brooklyn. Initially, my parents did not want me to move there, but they realized that it was solely my decision. I was now grown (haha). I was still braiding hair and had maintained a regular clientele and was earning a decent income as a young adult. However, for nearly two years, I had to travel back home every weekend to braid hair and earn a living, which my mother and father were happy about because they were able to check on me with regularity.

Meanwhile, in New York and not sure what I wanted to do with my life, I figured I would enroll in cosmetology school and get my state license. I attended the then Robert Fiance Hair Design Institute of New York. The nine-month program turned into fifteen months because while I was in cosmetology school, I received a call from internationally renowned recording Gloria Gaynor to braid her hair and later traveled with her to South America and Europe as her assistant, which was my first introduction to the music industry.

After traveling internationally for a few months, I returned to Robert Fiance and finished school. Shortly thereafter, I was accepted into an apprenticeship program in the coloring department at the prestigious Vidal Sassoon Hair Salon, then located on Fifth Avenue, less than a block away from both the landmark Plaza Hotel and The Sherry Netherland Hotel. I recall conversations with the school faculty, and I expressed my desire to work at Vidal Sassoon. Many of the students and some of the faculty thought that I was overreaching and that maybe I should settle for a Black hair salon such as the John Atchison Hair Salon. John was a successful Black hairstylist and entrepreneur, a former employee of Vidal Sassoon, and the first Black hairstylist that came out of the elite New York shop. He later became my mentor. While I listened to the naysayers, I was determined to go work at Vidal Sassoon. When I went for my interview at the famed salon, I showed the managers the portfolio of my braid designs and they were so impressed with my talent, I was hired immediately.

The clientele of the shop were progressive New Yorkers with high-earning potential, who always gave great tips. Occasionally, Mr. Sassoon would come to the shop to get groomed, and it was always a big deal when he visited. One day, I was assigned to wash his hair. I was so nervous; I will never forget when he told me that I had a "nice touch." That moment made my day, and I was on cloud nine for months.

During my tenure there, I was the only Black apprentice and there were no other Black hairstylists on staff. Many of my colleagues thought I would go in the same direction as John Atchison. During my nearly two years at Vidal Sassoon, I realized that I was finished with the braiding and hairstyling business altogether, I no longer had a desire for the profession. The teachable moment for me was to always shoot high and start from the top down. To this day, I often refer to that experience and it has served as a reminder and reinforcement when it was time to make key decisions.

After Vidal Sassoon, still not firm on my career goals, I wanted to seek out opportunities in television. I applied for a position at ABC-TV, then Capital Cities, and was offered a position as a secretary in the Broadcast, Engineering, and Operations division of the company. This was during the height of the satellite evolution, before my work in the music industry, before PR, and before Disney. It was also during this time that I enrolled at the City University of New York's Baruch College. ABC-TV was one of my best employers and experiences. The corporation reimbursed employees if they attended college. I obtained considerable knowledge about broadcasting, business, the corporate work environment, and overall responsibility. It is also where I fell in love with News. After more than 30 years, I still have my checking account with the credit union.

In the mid-eighties, my career in the music industry officially started at ASCAP, known as the American Society of Composers, Authors, and Publishers, still located in the Lincoln Center area of the city. I worked in an entry-level position as an administrative assistant in the television department. It was before the era and expansion of broadcast cable networks, cell phones, the world wide web, social media, and digital downloads and streaming.

In the television department, we were responsible for ascertaining the number of music plays of theme songs and background music that were broadcast on television programs, which were later accrued and calculated into quarterly royalty payments to music composers and publishers. I was assigned to many of the television shows I watched as a child that became reruns on local television stations across the country. In the beginning, I often wondered why these music creators were still getting paid for a television show that was created two-three decades earlier. I soon learned about the power of music and the business of music, which helped me to understand the foundation of the music and recording industries.

After three or more years at ASCAP, I had a series of other employment opportunities including my work as a personal assistant to supermodel Beverly Johnson. I worked as a temp at several law firms, where I built strong administrative skills. I also continued taking courses at Baruch and later at the New School.

One day, I met Jacqueline Rhinehart, who at the time was working with Charles Huggins' music management company, HUSH Productions. She was living in Brooklyn and was looking for a roommate to share the rent and space. I was living in East Harlem with my great-aunt, and I was ready for a move and change. We didn't know each other that well, but we had some of the same mutual friends and business associates. She convinced me to move in and share the space with her and her brother, William Rhinehart. We lived in a beautiful duplex, four-bedroom apartment, located in the historic district of Clinton Hill in Brooklyn, where Spike Lee, Wesley Snipes, Wynton Marsalis, Branford Marsalis, Rosie Perez, Chris Rock, Terence Blanchard, Lisa Cortes, Donald Harrison, Wendell Pierce, Nelson George, Leroy Campbell, and so many others resided. Clinton Hill reminded me of the modern-day Black Belt of the late 1880s, where well-to-do Black people lived and prosper. The neighborhood was a secure, warm, and family environment.

Ready to figure out the next steps and secure employment at a record label, Jackie, as many affectionally referred to her, secured a plum position as the Director of Artist Development at Mercury Records, under the leadership of Ed Eckstein. Still, my roommate, Jackie offered me a position as a publicity coordinator at Mercury Records, under the PolyGram corporation, I finally secured my first job at a major record company. The label's roster included Tony! Toni! Toné, Brian McKnight, Oleta Adams, Vanessa Williams, Third World, Jon Lucien, Black Sheep, Ed O. G. & Da Bulldogs, and other emerging artists. The staff included Tony Anderson, Lisa Cortes, Leighton Singleton, David Gossett, Gary Beach, Bob Duckett, Sandy Lawrence, Thornell Jones Jr., Walter Greene, Ron Carter, and of course our fierce leader, Jackie.

Within that year, I lost my first job at Mercury Records due to a bad attitude. I was officially in the record industry.

Sad, depressed, and broke, I had to return to temp work. I secured a long-term assignment for more than two years at Coudert Brothers, a then-top-level international law firm. Additionally, I took on several independent PR assignments at different neighborhood establishments in Brooklyn.

Nearly three years later, Jackie called me one day and asked me if I was interested in a job at Flavor Unit, and I said, "I don't want to work for an all-rap label." Her follow-up was, "You don't have a job in the industry and no one is calling."

Shakim Compere, who co-founded Flavor Unit Management and Flavor Unit Records called Jackie to see if she was interested in the job, but she had just accepted a position with Hiriam Hicks' management company in Philadelphia.

Shortly thereafter, I accepted the position, and I was named National Director of Publicity for Flavor Unit Entertainment. I enjoyed my four-to-five-year tenure there, commuting daily from Brooklyn to

Jersey City. I also handled video promotions and some marketing for the four-person staff label, which included president Charm Warren, Kobie Brown, the late Glenn "G-Man" Holt, and myself. Both Queen Latifah and Shakim gave me room to grow and the opportunity to set my path. Shakim is a visionary beyond his years. The label and management roster included Naughty By Nature, D-Nice, Zhané, Black Sheep, Freddie Foxx, Fu-Schnickens, Apache, Nikki D, LeShaun, Latee Shabazz, Almighty RSO, and Bigga Sistas.

Through the years, Jackie has single-handedly been responsible for most of my mid-level to executive positions at the record labels including Mercury Records, Flavor Unit Records, Island Records (Island Black Music), and Arista Records.

After Flavor Unit in 1995, I made a lateral move to Capitol Records and worked mainly with R&B and legacy artists and soundtrack projects including BeBe & CeCe, The Whispers, Rachelle Ferrell, Portrait, Jesse Campbell, and Tracie Spencer. That was also during the time that BeBe & CeCe parted ways as a duo to record solo projects. I worked on CeCe's first solo album, *Alone In His Presence.*

At Capitol Records, my office was across the hall from Blue Note Records where the legendary music man Bruce Lundvall headed the label. He introduced me to many jazz projects. He would always hand deliver advanced copies of the music on the upcoming releases. He once gifted me with a Mosaic Records' Nat King Cole Trio 18-CD box set, which I still have to this day. He was a great man; always kind and gentle.

In 1996, after only one year, Capitol Records disbanded its Urban Music division, one week before the 38th Annual Grammy Awards. I was out of work again. I was scheduled to attend the awards ceremony with CeCe, who was nominated in the Best Contemporary Soul Gospel Album category for *Alone In His Presence.* In addition, there was a performance with CeCe, Whitney Houston, and Shirley Caesar, backed by Hezekiah Walker and the Love Fellowship Choir. In that same segment, Brandy and Michael W. Smith presented the Gospel category and CeCe won. In her acceptance speech, she thanked me for working on that project and that night my phone rang off the hook.

One of those calls was from Jackie, who attended that year's Grammy Awards and was in the lobby of the Shrine Auditorium in Los Angeles talking to Hiriam Hicks about hiring me for a job. After Jackie's persuasion, and CeCe's remarks from the stage, I had a signed contract the following week, along with a salary increase and a new title, Senior Director of Publicity at Island Records' Black Music. Founded by Rock and Roll Hall of Famer Chris Blackwell, Island Records' label roster included the Isley Brothers, who were also Rock and Roll Hall of Fame inductees, R&B act Dru Hill and Gospel legend Karen Clark Sheard.

Six months into the new position at Island, I was ready to leave. One day, Jackie and I were on the phone, and she was ready to leave Arista to take on a new marketing position, and I was ready to leave Island Black Music. She then asked me if I wanted to interview for her position as Senior Director of Publicity. I said, "Hell yeah." She set up a meeting with me and her then-boss, Michele Mena, now Michelle Cucci.

I was still under contract with Island Records; I sneaked over to Arista to conduct the interview. I wore my big fur coat, and my big hair, and Michele later told me when she first saw me, she knew I was the right person for the position. However, Arista could not offer me a position until I was released from my contract with Island Records. Once that was done, Arista officially offered me a job. Jackie was released from her contract with Arista, and she accepted a position with Universal Records as the Vice President of Marketing.

I signed my new contract with Arista Records as the Senior Director of Publicity in December 1996 with a start date of January 1997. I secured a significant salary increase and was looking forward to working with some of my favorite A-list artists including Aretha Franklin and Whitney Houston. My roster also included Deborah Cox, Monica, Diddy, Faith Evans, Mase, and others.

Arista was my dream job and I loved working there. Through the years, I maintained many close relationships with some of my former colleagues. I learned so much from Clive Davis and the senior executive team there. I am forever grateful for his leadership and for creating an atmosphere of winning. I had the opportunity to work and be among some of the best executives in the music industry.

In 2001, Roy Lott, then the president of Capitol Records, and Michele Cucci, who later moved over to Capitol from Arista, offered me a position to serve a second tenure at "The House That Nat [King Cole] Built," as Vice President of Publicity in the Urban Music division. I accepted the position and then it happened again. One month after 9/11, Capitol Records dismantled the Urban Music division and that was my last label job.

The following year in 2002, I started my independent publicity and public relations firm GQ Media & Public Relations, Inc. (now Gwendolyn Quinn Public Relations). Our first client was EMI Gospel recording artists Shirley Murdock and Smokie Norful. My first marquee signing was Aretha Franklin.

In retrospect, my decision to start GQ Media & Public Relations was probably one of the best career decisions I made. Though I made numerous mistakes and I failed occasionally, it also forced me to grow, think and create outside of the proverbial box. My goal was to establish a full-service publicity and marketing firm that specializes in developing media strategies and coordinating special events and brand development for clients who span the worlds of entertainment, performing arts (theatre), corporate, not-for-profit, faith-based, and the visual/fine arts.

In 2001, I created a platform and formed the African American Public Relations Collective (AAPRC) to fill the gap in the networking potential among African American public relations and media specialists working in the communications field. The AAPRC was a national and international group of more than 1,000 public relations and communications specialists that provided professional support to their peers in the communications industry. We shared special event information, employment leads, career development resources, and vital links to media opportunities.

The AAPRC associates represented a wide range of fields including music, television, film, performing arts (theater and dance), fine/visual arts (painters, sculptors, etc.), sports, brand development, book and magazine publishing, fashion and beauty, corporate, education, community relations/affairs, healthcare, government, non-profit organizations, faith-based organizations, special events, politics, independent public relations firms, and other specialized areas.

As a brand extension of the AAPRC, we launched *The AAPRC Monthly* in February 2004, now titled *Global Communicator*, which was relaunched in June 2020, via the *Medium.com* platform. *Global Communicator* is an e-publication for African American public relations, marketing, journalists, and communications professionals.

If I had not made the key decision to step out on my own, I would have never been able to develop and expand my gifts, resources, and my natural and creative talents.

Gwendolyn Quinn with client Deborah Cox

Acknowledgments

This book is my personal love letter to:

All the Sheroes in Music and who came before me and gave me a seat at the table.

All the Sheroes who worked beside me, working with you gave me so much joy and pride.

All the Sheroes to whom we have collectively passed the baton --we see you and we celebrate you.

The women who have worked behind the scenes in music are deserving of their flowers while they are here. They are worthy of having their contributions and achievements acknowledged accurately and truthfully. This book is wrapped in a bouquet, this the beginning of a Movement, the forthcoming Docu-Series will be their flowers.

I would like to express my deep, deep gratitude to my co-creator and co-founder Dr. LaJoyce Brookshire. Thank you for always believing in my crazy, and for loving me and supporting me every step of the way. We been making "good trouble" in these streets for 20+ years, so cheers to another 20!

To my sister and parent publisher Elissa Gabrielle, thank you. Thank you for seeing our vision. Thank you for your support. Thank you for standing with us to tell our stories. We know how personal this project is to you as the daughter of the late, great Mike Bernardo. And while she is not here to get her flowers, we look forward to telling her story and honoring her legacy. I hope we have made her proud.

I would also like to express my deepest gratitude to all the contributors of the *Women Behind The Mic* Book Volume One. Thank you for believing in this project, thank you for sharing your stories with me and with the world. Thank you for your unwavering support. Reading through all the submissions I once again found myself in awe. Sisters you do indeed *Shine bright like a Diamond*! Your willingness to share your personal stories of triumph, set-backs, life lessons, and so much more have made this Movement and project a reality.

To my late Papa Bear, thank you for telling Mommy to 'leave me be' when she about had a heart attack about my going into the entertainment business. Thank you for encouraging me to dream big. I know that I made you proud because you told me that I did.

To my Mama Bear, thank you for exposing me to music, the arts, and culture at such a young age. You were the one that fanned the flames of my creativity, you taught me to pursue my dreams with passion and with purpose. I rose because you taught me how to fly.

To my bestie Gini: You are the sister that I never had, you have been with me through good and bad, ups and downs, wins and lessons. I cannot imagine my life without you. You are and always will be the yin to my yang. You are and will always be my perfect Partner In Crime.

To my brothers IW and Hezues, thank you for always having my back and for 'seeing' me, being appreciative of my work, and I will say again for ALWAYS having my back. We may not be related by blood, but you are my family.

To all my friends who never tire of hearing me talk about this project, I thank you. To all my friends who rallied around me when life happened and encouraged me to get back at it, I thank you.

Today my heart is full, I am excited for what lies ahead.

Thank you to everyone who helped us bring this project to fruition!

And finally, a heartfelt thank you to every one of our readers, your interest and your support is truly humbling.

Be Inspired.

With Love,
~MJ

I begin first with a thank you to the Lord God Almighty just as I do when I crack my eyes open and before closing them at night. Thank you, Lord, for giving me an ear to hear, the eyes to see, the desire to acknowledge an assignment, and an ability for project execution. Apart from you I can do nothing.

I want to extend a huge Thank You to the women who contributed to this body of work. I know this writing was cathartic - dragging out a lot of memories both exhilarating and painful. For these reasons I am grateful you put pen to paper, or fingers to keyboard in sharing your contributions to Pop Culture. We are Sisters bonded together forever in the Culture!

To Michelle Joyce—my MJ: thank you for the endless conversations about this project and its need, beginning with our first session filled with complaints about the industry, and ending with the evidence of this completed work. You are more than a business partner—you are my Sister for life and my Sister in Christ. It has been the "MJ/LJ Show" getting work done for more than two decades and I know we will ride our partnership into our Golden Years.

To Lonai Mosely: We have been Sisters since the mid-80s savoring pots of collard greens and putting our money together for meals when money was tight, when we were both trying to gain a foothold within the entertainment industry. We have gone from holding each other down when we had no job, to sharing ONE job, from having temp jobs, to even being executives. I *know* the work you have put in to attain Executive Producer status, and I am so happy to work with you on all of our *WOMEN BEHIND THE MIC* Live events.

Elissa Gabrielle: My little Sis and publisher extraordinaire. Thank you for believing in my content repository enough to say YES to my publishing company Renewing Your Mind Ink being an imprint of your Peace in The Storm Publishing. I find it incredibly serendipitous that we are working together and your mom, the fabulous Mike Bernardo, was a champion for me in my early days working in the industry. I cannot wait to share how she ushered me into the fold! There are many more stories ahead for us to release…Let's get it.

To my Team of Brothers who make all things "GO" in my orbit Thank Youuuu! Irvin Wright (IW) my Supervising Producer who keeps all the wheels turning; Christopher Green who oversees every gadget to make it all go (because I promise I do NOT know which button to push); Elijah Muhammad my Photographer Extraordinaire who has taken the best shots ever of me and my events; Robert Bennet who keeps invaders out of my website; Paul Muhammad who is available for any website change, anytime; and Harry Lawson of Enigma Graphics who BRILLIANTLY created this book cover from a conversation and a couple of raggedy samples. Thank you for being in my head when I attempt to talk through an idea on book covers and flyers.

Sharel Gordon Love—Thank you for the wonderful editing. You never disappoint!

Jessica Tilles—You are certainly the best layout editor EVER. Thank you for manifesting my vision.

Madyson Burton—Thank you so much for your beautiful hand-drawn rendering of *WOMEN BEHIND THE MIC* on the inside of this book. You created this picture from just a few words I shared about a vision back when you were a high schooler in 2017. I am delighted that your work is on display as promised in this work.

Brooke Brookshire—My Angel Baby—Thank you for being my eyes and ears on the 'pulse' of what your generation needs, wants, and hates! I am so happy that you have had a front row seat to watch your "Tee Tees" in our Village unfold Black Girl Magic on this project. You have become exceptionally magical too! Mommy loves you!

Gus Brookshire—Thank you for being my Rock and for keeping me balanced. You have been able to talk me down in times when I wanted to quit, reason with me when I was ready to do battle, and you always offer a perspective I have not considered. Thank you for keeping up with our baby pooch Hunter and asking me if I want to eat when I have forgotten to feed myself and you. Who loves you Bay-Ba!

To My Mommie Joana Hunter-Baker: I know you are beaming Heavenly vibes my way. I feel the love and your watchful eye. This is my first published work since you have gone home to heaven in April 2022 and your absence is overwhelming. With every accomplishment in my life, thank you for always saying, "I'm so proud of you!", while you were here. I will always cherish knowing you were proud and hearing you say those words. I love you Mommie. See you later.

To the Reader: Thank you so much for your purchase, it will help to keep the Movement alive. Please share this book with every dreamer you know.

~Much Love…LaJoyce

CPSIA information can be obtained
at www.ICGtesting.com
Printed in the USA
LVHW021732070323
741120LV00002B/288